THE Art OF Pastoring

MINISTRY *WITHOUT* ALL THE ANSWERS

DAVID HANSEN

INTERVARSITY PRESS
DOWNERS GROVE, ILLINOIS 60515

InterVarsity Press® is the book-publishing division of InterVarsity Christian Fellowship®, a student movement active on campus at hundreds of universities, colleges and schools of nursing in the United States of America, and a member movement of the International Fellowship of Evangelical Students. For information about local and regional activities, write Public Relations Dept., InterVarsity Christian Fellowship, 6400 Schroeder Rd., P.O. Box 7895, Madison, WI 53707-7895.

Cover photograph: Dennis Frates

ISBN 0-8308-1669-0

Printed in the United States of America ∞

Library of Congress Cataloging-in-Publication Data

Hansen, David, 1953-
      The art of pastoring: ministry without all the answers/David Hansen.
         p.   cm.
      Includes bibliographical references.
      ISBN 0-8308-1669-0
      1. Pastoral theology.   2. Clergy—Office.   I. Title.
   BV4011.H33   1994
   253—dc20   94-409
                                                         CIP

17   16   15   14   13   12   11   10   9   8   7   6
08   07   06   05   04   03   02   01   00

Acknowledgments

This book springs from my experience as pastor of the Florence-Victor Parish in the Bitterroot Valley of Montana, from January 1983 to April 1992. My stories are set in small towns, ranch country and mountain wilderness. But this is not a book about rural ministry. My goal all along has been to write a book that describes pastoral ministry everywhere, in its many and diverse settings. I have simply believed that the best way to make a comprehensive statement about the pastorate is to describe its manifestation in a very specific context. Generalities about the pastoral ministry, designed to apply everywhere, may, after all, apply nowhere. But if a description of pastoral ministry in rural Montana strikes home with a pastor in an urban ministry thousands of miles away, then maybe we have struck pay dirt!

So I knew that I needed ministers in other places to read my manuscript to see if my stories and ideas connected with them. My readers have helped me immensely. Besides giving me much-needed encouragement along the way, they have corrected me at many points. Their critique has helped me write a better book. Of course I take full responsibility for the book's shortcomings.

These persons have read the manuscript in whole or in part: Steve Trotter, pastor of First Presbyterian Church, Ellensburg, Washington; Evelyn Breese, pastor of Southside United Protestant Church, Richland, Washington; Rob Cahill, student at Fuller Theological Seminary; Camille Richardson, student at Bethel Theological Seminary; Jim Steiner, pastor of Second Baptist Church, Boise, Idaho; Steve Yamaguchi, pastor of Grace Presbyterian Church, Paramount, California; Gaylord Hasselblad, executive minister for the American Baptist Churches of the Northwest; Alan Poole, associate pastor at Blacknall Presbyterian Church, Durham, North Carolina; Lois Halls, missionary to Guatemala; Bruce Becker, pastor of Olney Presbyterian Church, Philadelphia; Steve Mathewson, pastor of

Dry Creek Bible Church, Dry Creek, Montana; Dick McNeely, campus pastor at Montana State University and pastor of Springhill Presbyterian Church; Bill Stevenson, a writer, Cambridge, Massachusetts; Tim Fearer, pastor of Westminster Presbyterian Church, Port Hueneme, California; Mike Burr, pastor of United Church of Moscow, Moscow, Idaho; Thomas Elson, pastor of First Presbyterian Church, Lindsay, California; Bill Welch, pastor of Sierra Vista Presbyterian Church, Oakhurst, California; and Dave Dooley, chemistry professor at Montana State University, Belgrade.

I wish to thank the people of the Florence-Victor Parish. It was their burden to live with a young man in his earliest attempt to answer the call of God to be a pastor. They performed their task with sensitivity and understanding.

Finally, I wish to thank Debbie. She is a woman of deep justice, profound courage and the grace to take life lightly. In our twenty years as husband and wife, she has been a constant source of wisdom and freedom. This book is dedicated to her as a token of my gratitude, respect and love.

*There is a river whose streams
make glad the city of God.*

P S A L M   4 6 : 4

An Ebenezer Story: Introduction

This book is a description of the pastoral ministry. In it I attempt to answer questions such as, when the pastoral ministry happens,

☐ what does it look like?
☐ what does it feel like?
☐ what is it?

My answers come from the inside out. I have not studied the pastoral ministry from a dispassionate, objective standpoint. I have written as an interested party. I have written from the subjective standpoint of being a pastor.

When I began pastoral ministry, I had lots of books prescribing pastoral ministry—the so-called how-to books. I had books on how to preach, how to administrate a church, how to do pastoral counseling and how to lead small groups. They didn't help me. The authors assumed too much. They assumed that I knew what my goal was. They assumed that I knew what I was and who I was. They assumed that I knew why I was supposed to be doing the things they were teaching me about. But I didn't know what I was, or who I was, or why I was supposed to be doing the things I was supposed to be doing. And I didn't know how any of the things I was supposed to be doing fit into a coherent understanding of my call from God to be a pastor.

So I stopped reading how-to books. Instead I read theology, biblical studies and church history. I alternated between the disciplines. These books from the classical disciplines of theology didn't teach me how to do pastoral ministry, but they helped me immensely in my regular duties. I discovered that spending a day reading thirty pages of Karl Barth's *Dogmatics* helped me more in my pastoral work than a hundred of pages of how-to literature.

In my church history reading I ran into a biography of a pastor, *The Life of Alexander Whyte;* a personal narrative of a pastor, *The Letters of Samuel Rutherford;* and a fictional account of a pastor, Father Zossima in Feodor Dostoyevsky's *The Brothers Karamazov.* Alexander Whyte, who finished his long career in the early part of the twentieth century, pastored a large church in Scotland. Samuel Rutherford, a Scottish pastor from the 1600s, wrote his letters during times of persecution. Father Zossima is a portrayal of a Russian monk of the 1800s.

These books helped me a lot. But I didn't know why stories about pastors who lived centuries ago could help me so much. I thought I was supposed to be a modern pastor, relevant to the world around me; and these books were from different worlds. But as I read these stories I felt myself caught up in the protagonists' struggles to follow Jesus Christ in their daily lives.

These narratives pointed me to the fact that pastoral ministry is a life, not a technology. How-to books treat pastoral ministry like a technology. That's fine on one level—pastoral ministry does require certain skills, and I need all the advice I can get. But my life as a pastor is far more than the sum of the tasks I carry out. It is a call from God that involves my whole life. The stories I read helped me to understand my life comprehensively. My life, too, is a story, and it is the narrative quality of my life that makes my ministry happen. Others see and participate in the story as it is told. I have discovered that when I follow Jesus in my everyday life as a pastor, people meet Jesus through my life.

This is not a new idea. It is a simple observation, perhaps the most basic principle of evangelism, that we lead people to Christ through living simple lives of love.

What is new about this book is that I attempt to describe *why* it is that people meet Jesus in our lives when we follow Jesus. Even more, I have attempted to describe how and why following Jesus is the central principle of pastoral ministry, the comprehensive principle that integrates every task.

The thesis of this book is that people meet Jesus in our lives because when we follow Jesus, we are parables of Jesus Christ to the people we meet. This book is a description of the pastor as a parable of Jesus Christ.

Since this book is about the pastoral ministry as a narrative, the book itself is a narrative, the story of my life as a pastor. It is, specifically, the story of my life as pastor of the Florence-Victor Parish, a two-church, yoked parish in the Bitterroot Valley of Montana, which I served from January 1983 to April 1992.

This book contains more than the story of my nine-year pastorate. As I attempted to describe and understand my life as a pastor, I was forced again and again to refer to other experiences in my life. For instance, I found that I had no choice but to describe my conversion experience.

This raises the question of why my conversion story—or any story I tell about myself—should have any relevance to you and your ministry. By recounting my conversion experience, I do not want to imply that you must have had a conversion experience like mine in order to be a pastor. What I do want to imply is that your conversion has great implications for your ministry. Just as I have looked carefully into my conversion experience (and many of my stories) to understand my ministry, you must also look carefully at your conversion experience (and many of your stories) to understand *your* ministry.

That's the beautiful thing about narrative. As you read my investigation of my experience of ministry, you are not asked to duplicate my experience of ministry. Rather, you are invited to investigate your experience of your ministry. As I tug you through my exploration, I hope that you will be doing exploration too.

This book is a weaving of stories and didactic sections. Pay attention to both equally. But realize that I have given priority to the stories. Do not hurry through them. The didactic sections illustrate the stories, rather than the reverse.

I apologize for the places in the book where you will be slowed down because my writing is poor. I am deeply aware of my shortcomings as a writer, and I wish I could have made it easier for you. On the other hand, I do not apologize for the fact that the pastoral ministry is filled with sticky, complex problems that can only be addressed with sticky, complex writing. I find that I cannot write an easy book about a hard subject. I only hope the book is not harder than the subject matter deserves!

Obviously this book is for pastors. But it is not just for pastors. I sincerely hope that this book can meet the needs of two other groups in the church.

If you are considering entering the pastoral ministry, this book will give you a glimpse of what it is like to be a pastor. I don't think how-to books can help you see and feel the life of ministry. I doubt that even the best book on how to preach a sermon can help you know what it is like to preach a sermon. This book, I hope, can help you feel what it is like to preach a sermon.

If you are a layperson, active in a church, and you want to know what your pastor is going through, this book may help you to understand. These days there is a gap between laypeople and pastors. Laypeople don't know what pastors do. Most of us pastors don't know what we're doing either. These are difficult times for us.

I'll admit, too often we pastors just gripe. You may be justifiably tired of listening to our bellyaching. But sometimes your expectations for our ministries are askew. Sometimes you want things from us that we just can't deliver.

The great missing element in today's relationships between pastors and laypeople is trust. Trust comes from love and understanding. I warmly invite you to come into this narrative as one of us. Walk in our shoes for a little while.

It needs to be said that your pastor may not believe everything I write here, and you should not judge your pastor by what I say. (Then again, you may be *glad* that your pastor's opinions don't always match mine.)

Finally, this book is an Ebenezer. Scripture says: "Then Samuel took a stone and set it up between Mizpah and Shen. He named it Ebenezer, saying, 'Thus far has the LORD helped us' " (1 Sam 7:12). This was not an uncommon practice in early Israel. The patriarchs piled up rocks to mark where the Lord had met them. They made altars where they thanked God for what he had done for them. Afterward, when they walked by the rock piles on their pilgrimages, the rocks served as reminders of God's faithfulness. This book is a pile of rocks declaring that God has helped me along the way in my wilderness walk as a pastor.

By writing this book I am not claiming to have been a good pastor. All I claim—and this seems bold enough to me—is that I have been a pastor. I have failed many times. Many times I have violated my own best precepts of pastoral ministry. As I look back on my ministry I do not see my faithfulness. What I see is God's faithfulness. My performance has been mixed. God is the one that has been faithful at every point. My faithfulness, to the extent that I have been faithful, has had its roots in God's faithfulness to the people he has called me to serve.

It is a great mystery to be a pastor. To the memory of God's faithful and mysterious work I have stacked these rocks.

1

Beginning

He who receives you receives me,
and he who receives me
receives the one who sent me.

MATTHEW 10:40

*M*y face sinks into my hands, but the desk is too cold for my elbows. The space heater with the cloth-covered cord has warmed the air: my breath doesn't show, but the steel desk warms excruciatingly slowly. It's freezing me. I'm too cold to read a book.

My office is a lean-to attachment to the fellowship hall of a community church in rural Montana. There's no wall heater, no thermostat, no insulation. The place warms from scratch every morning. It's six weeks into the new year, six weeks into my first pastoral charge, 33 degrees outside and sleeting.

It's sleeting in my soul. I don't know what I'm supposed to do. I've been called, educated, interned and ordained. I have learned lists of tasks to do, but not what I am to *be*. I'm cold and afraid. There are a hundred things I could do if I could just stop shivering.

In the spring skunks seek secluded dens to make skunk love and raise skunklings. Our fellowship hall, with its crumbling stone foundation, extends a warm invitation to them. Its gaping holes say more than words ever could: "We welcome you to this church."

We are a family church. We attempt to provide what young couples are looking for. And we've never met a family's needs better than we've met the Skunks'. Our crawl space is dark and dry, and the trash cans outside the door are perpetually knocked over by wandering dogs. A healthy Montana skunk smells like a burning tire. The acrid odors wafting through my office in springtime make me appreciate the pure 33-degree air I inhale in the winter.

While conjugating a Greek verb, I hear gnawing from the crawl space. I stomp; the noise stops. I return to the Greek, and the noise resumes.

Maybe I should have demanded decent working conditions. But after a while I realized something: my office conditions delivered me from the temptation of seeking a job description from the church. I knew what they wanted from me: competent pastoral care and leadership, regular office hours and good preaching. I was hoping to meet these reasonable expectations. But I knew that I couldn't let the church tell me who I was or how I should go about my work. After all, they couldn't even see that I needed a heater in my office. I began to question my situation.

Do I deserve a heater in my office?

Yes, I do.

Are these cheap, meanhearted people?

No, they pay me pretty well. I like these people.

Why don't they do something about my office?

I don't know.

Do they have the slightest idea what I do?

No, they don't.

Do I want people who provide me with an office in which I face hypothermia in the winter and asphyxiation in the spring to tell me who I am and what I should be doing?

No, I do not.

After a couple of years the space heater broke (kicked over too many times, I guess), and I did get a wall heater. But the floor never collapsed, so the foundation was never fixed and the skunks stayed. I put up with the situation because it showed me that while I serve the church, I do not work for the church. I never wanted to become their employee, and I never did. What I became was their pastor.

My employer is Jesus Christ. Serving the church is my obedient response to Christ. Jesus is my boss; he orders my day. Shivering while preparing my sermons forced me to take seriously who I was preparing my sermons for: Jesus Christ—who also had no place to rest his elbows. The church got better sermons because of it.

Trend-Driven Ministry

My predecessor's library haunted me. When he left this church, he left the ministry and forsook his library. Every single book remained in the office on the shelves, undisturbed; he took not one. My library was shelved in my other office in the other church, so his books stayed in place, like Little Boy Blue's toy soldiers obediently waiting for their master.

His library told the story of his ministry. The books were ordered in topical fashion, but instead of "Pastoral Counseling" and "Commentaries" his topics represented most of the trends of Christianity in the 1970s, the decade of his pastoral ministry.

He had some highly conservative commentaries, Bible introductions, a systematic theology, some charts of the end times and "Christian counseling" books.

The church growth movement was well represented. He went to some conferences on the subject and bought books. Church minutes from his tenure reveal that council members attended the conferences with him. They also reveal that he tried the methods but with no results. Closets, desk drawers and file cabinets were filled with dittos of church growth teaching materials, church surveys and proposals.

He journeyed as a charismatic. Books on healing, speaking in tongues and discovering spiritual gifts were present and dog-eared to prove they'd been read.

He had learned from books how to organize growth groups and spiritual retreats.

Social action literature from evangelical, Mennonite and Catholic sources took up space, including several years' worth of subscriptions to journals dedicated to social concern and Christian sarcasm. From late in his ministry there was a smattering of literature from Reformed theology, psychology, liberal theology and biblical studies.

A few parishioners told me with deep sadness that by the end of his ministry he had lost much of his Christian faith. His faith crisis did his ministry in. The books couldn't deliver him.

He was a fine pastor. Everyone said he was a good preacher. He was tireless at calling, superb at organizing small groups. I was amazed at how many parishioners from different age groups and backgrounds gave him this high tribute: "He was a real friend to me."

He did good work through all the years of trying one movement and then another. He pastored well whether he happened to be a dispensationalist, a charismatic, a small group organizer, a church growth enthusiast or a social activist. The movements he followed actually had little if any effect on his ministry, except in a fatal way: ultimately perhaps he confused following Christian movements with following Christ.

Most of the books and articles were written by genuine Christians. What went wrong?

I didn't know what went wrong. His library presented a bleak testimony to me, though. He and I were cut from the same piece of cloth. I believed that following Christian movements amounted to following Christ. I was suckled on trend-driven Christianity. I'd grown up in the thick of consumer religion. It was all I knew. I knew every movement represented in his library. I'd tried them all myself. I didn't know if I could do pastoral ministry without them. But every time I looked up at his library, I knew that I had to try.

Task-Driven Ministry

Meanwhile, in order to survive, I was performing my tasks as a pastor with as much skill and energy as I could. I preached, taught Bible studies, prayed, led worship and administered the sacraments. I pastored the people as best I could. To my surprise, the churches didn't fire me. They liked my work. I wasn't following a job description or a Christian movement. My ministry was task-driven. I organized every day around accomplishing jobs I assigned myself.

Task-driven ministry has some advantages. It keeps the church going. It pays the rent. It's real life. Which is a lot more than can be said for fad-driven ministry.

I really think that task-driven ministry comes from academic theology. Look for pastoral ministry in any systematic theology. Many don't mention it. Those that do mention it treat only what pastors *do.*

For instance, every good Christian theology devotes a large section to the preaching of the Word of God. Pastors may be mentioned in passing as preachers. An equally large section belongs to the sacraments. The author may mention that normally pastors administer the sacraments. Ethics are important, and are taught by pastors. Church order is important, and pastors oversee church order. The very justification for academic theology is that eventually its insights will reach the parish so pastors can do good ministry. Academic theology summarizes pastoral work this way: Pastors do things.

Professional theologians wonder why pastors don't read theology. The fault lies with them. Since theologians describe pastors as people who *do* things in the church, pastors don't have time to read theology. Since pastors are taught to be task doers, academic theology has sent pastors to the quick and lightweight how-to books. If theologians lament that pastors are not sufficiently interested in eschatology, it is because time management is the new eschatology. Theology's venerable "already and not yet" has become "what needs to be done today and what can be left until tomorrow."

Task-driven ministry always gives way to a time-management ministry as opposed to a Spirit-led ministry. The pastor's day is divided into hours and tasks rather than opportunities to do God's will. The problem is that when I fine-tune my week, tweaking it like a piano tuner to a perfect A440, I am out of harmony with the kingdom of God. I experience fewer of those serendipitous, perfect opportunities to talk to people about Christ. You know what I mean: the evangelism you never plan, which works better than evangelism you do plan.

The most insidious rationalization for a task-driven ministry is that it provides a pastor with a professional identity. A surgeon is a person trained and authorized to perform surgery. A teacher is a person trained and authorized to teach school. A pastor is a person trained and authorized to carry out pastoral tasks. As a professional, I am a person with expertise. Experts have esoteric knowledge with powers to accomplish tasks. Such knowledge makes us valuable to society. It separates me from those around me. I become "distinguished."

My ego loves the distance created by esoteric knowledge; it is the power of the witch doctor. But in the end the tragic distance created is within my own soul. When I move from being a lover of the soul to an expert about the soul, I objectify my own soul from myself. In the end my ego is warped; it goes on a rampage, climbing ladders to assert itself.

Better to be a follower of Jesus and no expert at that, just a sinner saved by grace, called to love because I have been bought with a price. I may lose my standing as an expert, but I gain my soul.

The pastoral ministry cannot be employer-driven, trend-driven or task-driven. Pastoral ministry must be following Jesus Christ. Jesus Christ called me to this work, and following him must be integral to realizing his calling.

How does following Jesus Christ accomplish the pastoral ministry?

Pastoral Ministry As Following Jesus Christ

It was one of those clear October afternoons in Montana when the leaves had turned but not fallen. The air was cool but the ground warm—a good day for seeing things. A good day for fishing.

The Bitterroot River riparian zone is a benign chaos of cottonwoods, high grasses, red willows, wild roses and some of the best dry fly fishing in Montana. The lack of order reminds me of my life. Birds float in and out like parishioners. Moist bear scat under a freshly stripped wild chokecherry tree reminds me to keep my eye open for danger. The Bitterroot River—clean, cold, fertile, always moving forward, always cutting new banks, providing constant nourishment for our valley—reminds me of the Holy Spirit. That we can pollute the river, dam it and reroute it reminds me that in my ministry I can quench the Holy Spirit.

I may see a beaver, a mink or a bald eagle, but this is not a nature hike. I'm fishing, and fishing is predation. I'm not watching nature, I'm joining it. My eyes survey the river for rising trout. My mind surveys the Spirit for new ideas.

I come upon a section of river notorious for large trout too wary to be caught. These fish rise eighteen inches from the shore in a pure glass slick. They rise so close to the bank they can see you. As usual, the big ones rise, slowly sipping tiny flies off the surface tension of the water. I hike upstream past the hole and hide behind a tree stump as I loosen my line. The small fly, a number 18 Yellow Humpy, meanders into the slough of feeding trout. A large cutthroat trout takes the fly.

The trout experiences something like death when he fights against the hook and line. The lactic acid builds up in his system and causes him a deep ache. Once the fish is in my hands I turn him upside-down, which disorients him, temporarily relaxing his muscles. I ease the hook out of his mouth, gently lowering him into the water facing upstream so his gills will fill with oxygen. He heads to the deep slowly, tired and sore. I know how he feels.

The fish returns to his place in the carefully defined order of trout-dom. I look for my place in Christendom. As I walk through the grasses I smell the sweet odor of decomposing plants. As I tramp through theology I smell dead matter too, but it isn't sweet. The typical response of the theologian is that "Pastoral Ministry" belongs under the rubric "Church." I see the point, of course: The church calls pastors to do the most important work of the church. Pastors exercise the means of grace entrusted to the church until the Lord's return. This says what I do, but it does not say what I am.

I serve the church, and I'm willing to do that. I knew when I started pastoral ministry that it meant serving the church to the point of dying. I just want to die for the right thing. I do not want to die for the church by going crazy with ten million things to do. But that's what theology seems to offer me: a correct theology of baptism, a correct theology of preaching, a correct theology of all kinds of things that I'm supposed to do. What does all that have to do with following Jesus?

The fishing's not that great. I've walked two miles for two fish. I come to the barbed-wire fence where I usually turn around and head for home. If I shimmy under it I'll probably rip my waders, or I may get chased by an angry landowner. But the time has come to explore new water. The waders rip, the fishing gets better, no angry landowner appears.

Jesus Is the Parable of God

I step over downed cottonwood tree trunks and force my way through tall grass, one eye out to keep me from tripping, the other eye on the river looking for good water.

How can I begin to think about the act of following Jesus as also being the act of doing the pastoral ministry? Jesus is the Image of God. Jesus is the Servant of God and is the Servant of the church. A pastor is made in the image of God. A pastor is a servant of God and is a servant of the church. Jesus is the Image of God and the Servant of the church to such an extent that in knowing Jesus we know God.

In Jesus we know God. When Christ is heard and received through Word and sacrament, God comes to us. In knowing Jesus we know God. This is the foundation of the Christian faith, and it must also be the foundation of the pastoral ministry. How can we describe how God comes to us today, through Jesus Christ?

Eberhard Jüngel says that Jesus is the parable of God. He says of this insight: "This christological statement is to be regarded as the fundamental proposition of a hermeneutic of the speakability of God."[1]

What is a parable? A parable is an extended metaphor. "The parable is regarded as an extended metaphor, or the metaphor can be called an abbreviated parable. The difference consists in the fact that a parable narrates while a metaphor coalesces the narrative in a single word."[2]

A parable is a story meant to create a comparison between a known thing and an unknown thing, the purpose being to illuminate the unknown thing so as to bring something new, unforeseen and surprising to the hearer. The story of Jesus is a parable of God because Jesus is a man and can be seen whereas God is Spirit and cannot be seen. Jesus' life is the story of God and God's love, and as we hear and believe the story of Jesus, God does come to us!

Jesus is the unique and authoritative Parable of God. There is no other human being that can bear this title. Trinitarian theology is essential to Christian thinking, preaching, teaching and prayer. Jesus of Nazareth is uniquely the Son of God and is the proper subject of preaching. It has been observed many times that when he preached, Jesus did not preach about himself but about God. In the totality of his life, he bore the image of God perfectly. But in order for us to tell the story of God, we must tell the story of Jesus' life, for only through Jesus do we know God. As the Parable of God, Jesus brings us God.

If it is true that in preaching Jesus we bring God to our people, perhaps in following Jesus in our daily lives we can bring God to people on the same principle. In other words, if Jesus is the Parable of God and preaching the story of Jesus brings God to people, if we live our lives following Jesus, maybe our lives can bring Jesus to people. Maybe we can be parables of Jesus.

The Pastor Is a Parable of Jesus Christ

There are many similarities between Jesus' life and a pastor's life. Jesus was called into ministry. He was anointed with the Holy Spirit for ministry. He underwent temptation from the devil. Jesus believed and taught that the consequences of how we live our lives extend into eternity. Jesus preached, he prayed, he befriended sinners, and he instituted the Lord's Supper and baptism. Jesus died for the world and for the church. The pastor undergoes all these things. It shouldn't surprise us that our lives are similar to Jesus' life. That is, after all, the whole point of being a disciple: following Jesus by doing what he did.

Jesus is the Parable of God and delivers God to us in the process. Isn't it possible that pastors, to the extent that they follow Jesus, are parables of Jesus Christ and so deliver him to those they encounter?

This is why when I walk into a hospital room, the people seem to experience the coming of God. Just to say it sounds egotistical. But sometimes on hospital calls, it is as if I am not even there. God is there. Sometimes God comes to people when I preach, or pray, or even when I'm just visiting with them. Being a parable of Jesus shows me how it is possibly true when he says: "He who receives you receives me, and he who receives me receives the one who sent me" (Mt 10:40).

Whenever Jesus' listeners received his parables, they were receiving him. When they rejected his parables, they were rejecting him. When they rejected him, they were rejecting God. That I can understand, because Jesus is himself the divine Son of God, and to reject him or his teaching is to reject God his Father. But how about me? How can listening to me be listening to Jesus? How can rejecting me be rejecting

Jesus and ultimately God? That becomes possible only when I am a parable of Jesus.

A man told me: "You don't know this, but before I became a Christian I used to avoid you on the street. You didn't even know who I was, but I knew who you were; when you'd come down the street, I'd duck out of the way. But the one I was really avoiding was God. He was the one I was running from. When I finally decided to start coming to church, and got to know you, I realized that I hadn't been running from you, I was running from God." So I also know what Jesus means when he says, "He who rejects you rejects me; but he who rejects me rejects him who sent me" (Lk 10:16).

Simply following Jesus is the greatest tool of evangelism. It makes us parables of Jesus.

I walk two hundred yards past the barbed wire. I'm on new water. It's invigorating. Exploring a segment of a river requires alertness. I screen sound: the water, the birds, my own footsteps. Listening for the anomaly, the splash out of place: the rise.

I scan the water to discern its rhythmic patterns. My eye looks for the sip, the splash, the fin, the fish's lips. I have to isolate the subtle rise (the big ones usually make the least splash) from the natural currents of the water.

What does a parable do?

I come upon a deep, quietly swirling sidewater pool. The pool tangents the main current. The speed of the main current causes the glassy water to spin slowly. Large trout hold in this kind of water. Food slides off the main current, entering the spinning pool. The trout wait in the quiet water as the placid current of the pool brings the food to them like a lazy susan.

I cast my home-tied, trout-bitten fly into the pool. The tricky currents of the whirlpool pull the line and the fly out of the trout's feeding lanes again and again. Finally one cast makes it. The feathers and thread cause a two-pound rainbow to rise and sip it in. Soon the fish is in my hands.

As a parable of Jesus Christ I deliver something to the parishioner that I am not, and in the process I deliver the parishioner into the hands of God.

I come to their home as I am. I am a known quantity to them. Because of my position as pastor, the family I visit knows from the start that something about God is happening. I listen to them tell their story, trying to keep my own Godforsaken ego-agenda out of the way. ("Why don't you come to church more often? I want a bigger church, and you're part of my plan.") After a while I pray for the family.

You wouldn't think that listening to people would be such a big deal. But listening to us is what God does. The fact that I listen to a family the way Jesus does makes a comparison happen inside them. A subconscious process tells them: *Jesus listens to me; this is what Jesus is like.* They sense they have been talking to Jesus all along.

Am I so desperate for identity that I've resorted to calling myself Jesus? No. I'm just a hook with some feathers and threads on it. I observe that when I encounter people along the way, they don't experience me so much as they experience God. How do I account for this? I am a parable of Jesus.

How else does Christ communicate himself through us to others? Seeing ourselves as parables of Jesus displaces the hazy, hyperspiritual gnostic spirituality that imagines God mystically seeping through us to others, ignoring our actual historical lives and bodies. The mystical seeping theory of sharing Jesus doesn't require ethics. In this view, who I am, what I am from day to day, doesn't really matter.

But if Jesus is communicated through us because of the likeness we share with him in our everyday life, if the essence of delivering Christ is living like him in our whole life, matching our life's narrative with his life's narrative, then our everyday life counts.

Every Christian's life is meant to be a parable of Jesus. But pastors are particularly suited to this, because so much of our lives are spent doing what Jesus did in his life. An adequate definition of pastoral ministry emphasizes following Jesus as the act of ministry, and particularly following Jesus on the way of the cross.

The Way of the Cross

In order to be parables of Jesus, we must pay close attention to two areas of his life: his ministry and the narrative of his life.

Jesus' ministry is so simple that most pastors consider it naive. Word. Prayer. Friendship. Sacrament. Leadership. That's all.

Jesus' life has a general narrative direction. We call this general direction the Way of the Cross. Jesus understood from the beginning that his was a life of sacrifice. His life flowed toward the cross at all times. He never climbed any first-century ladders of success. The devil showed him plenty. The people begged him to climb them. Jesus rejected ladders and consistently chose the downward road of sacrifice.

Furthermore, Jesus specifically directed us to follow him in his life's general direction, the Way of the Cross. Lest we object to bearing the cross as pietistic nonsense in a world of "scientific" management principles and psychological method, simply observe that virtually all the trouble that the best, most talented pastors get into comes from not following the Way of the Cross. The best and the most talented in the pastoral ministry and in denominational hierarchies harm themselves and harm the church most through their unrestrained ego and unwillingness to step off the high places. Sexual sin gets the press, but ego sin kills the church. Jesus told us exactly what direction our lives are to take: "If anyone would come after me, he must deny himself and take up his cross and follow me" (Mk 8:34).

The power to do pastoral ministry and its central focus, that which gives every aspect of it meaning, lies specifically in the everyday, concrete following of Jesus, led by him on the Way of the Cross. That is how we become parables of Jesus and deliver him to the people we meet. Paul recognized this when he told the Corinthians: "We always carry around in our body the death of Jesus, so that the life of Jesus may also be revealed in our body. For we who are alive are always being given over to death for Jesus' sake, so that his life may be revealed in our mortal body" (2 Cor 4:10-11).

No job description, no Christian movement or fad, no specific set of tasks always equals following Jesus. Yet once our life comes into line with the life of Jesus, we can borrow eclectically from many Christian movements and fads, we can take orders from ruling boards and even take on a time-effective task schedule!

Don't think that following Christ is hard. The pastoral ministry is much, much harder for those who do not deny themselves and pick up their cross. Jesus' words apply to us when he says, "Come to me, all you who are weary and burdened, and I will give you rest. Take my yoke upon you and learn from me, for I am gentle and humble in heart, and you will find rest for your souls. For my yoke is easy and my burden is light" (Mt 11:28-30).

Here's what the pastoral ministry is for me: Every day, as I go about my tasks as a pastor, I am a follower of Jesus. I am therefore a parable of him to those I encounter. The parable of Jesus works the power and presence of Jesus in their lives.

I am no more Jesus than a hook with feathers and threads is a mayfly. As I follow Jesus throughout my day, I fish for people for God. Ultimately what I am is the bait.

II

Call

It was he who gave some to be apostles,
some to be prophets, some to be evangelists,
and some to be pastors and teachers.

E P H E S I A N S   4 : 1 1

*G*od ties his own flies. As I look at my call to be a pastor, I feel
as if my life has been stuck in a vise and wound with a thread.

True fishermen prefer to fish with flies from their own vise. The fly
is the fisherman's logical, physical and spiritual extension. Custom flies,
tied to the specifications of a specific subspecies of aquatic insect, are
better bait than general patterns. A fly of my own creation better represents me to the monster I plumb the depths for.

To tie a fly, I first squeeze a bare hook in a vise. According to the
picture in my mind of the insect that lives in the river, I wind thread
around the hook to bind feathers and fur into place. The thread is pulled
so tight the strands threaten to snap at every turn. The result is the mug
of a bug, so convincing that my kid might take after it with a fly swatter.

Pastors are made by God to be pastors. It isn't a matter of our choosing. Pastors don't choose to be pastors any more than hooks and feathers

and threads choose to be a stonefly imitation. God chooses people to be pastors and makes them into pastors according to his plan.

Being a pastor is not just a matter of having a collection of pastoral spiritual gifts. Being a pastor is a gift all its own. "It was he who gave some to be apostles, some to be prophets, some to be evangelists, and some to be pastors and teachers" (Eph 4:11).

The Bible's elegant metaphor for God's servant-making is the womb. Jeremiah knew himself to be a prophet made in the womb. As God said to the young Jeremiah: "Before I formed you in the womb I knew you, before you were born I set you apart; I appointed you as a prophet to the nations" (Jer 1:5).

Knowing that I am made by God to be a pastor is my call. Next to my personal knowledge of Jesus Christ as Lord and Savior, it is my greatest possession. It keeps me on track in ministry. It keeps me from going crazy through all the ups and downs of parish life. It is my authorization to preach God's Word and administer the sacraments. It is my authorization to hear confession of sin and pronounce forgiveness. It is my assurance that God is my strength as I carry out my tasks. It is my glory, it is my cross. It is my election and my damnation.

Call is its own kind of knowledge. A call demands that it be known. It is a kind of information that contains within it the imperative that it be searched for and comprehended as if it were a matter of life and death.

Paul knew his call, gloried in it, struggled over it and suffered because of it. He wrote about it frequently. Jeremiah knew his call. He tried to shake it off but couldn't any more than he could shake off his own skin. Jonah knew his call and ran from it. In running from being the bait of God, he became food for a fish.

Knowing the call takes time. It begins with inklings about a road we sense we are being asked to take and ends with a deep knowing of one's self.

A few ciphers help me to understand the trail pastors take in knowing their call. They are

☐ hearing election and making covenant
☐ undergoing preparation and receiving a call
☐ knowing one's self as a pastor

Hearing Election and Making Covenant

Most of what I learned my freshman year of college I learned walking the streets of Salem, Oregon, and at a little country church on the edge of town.

I walked every afternoon. Study was impossible until I'd walked. In winter I walked the dark afternoons through the gray Pacific drizzling rain. I had an old corduroy coat and a white duster hat, and I didn't return to my dorm until I was soaked to the skin.

Eighteen years old, walking the streets of Salem, I searched my heart carefully. Inch by inch through every pleasure, every pain, all the dreamy ego trips (to use the proper historical nomenclature) and every hard reality, I reasoned my way through my soul. Once in a while I touched the image of God. The Spirit prayed through me as I looked at myself in God's presence and talked with him about what I was discovering.

My Christian friends and I attended a little American Baptist church on the outskirts of Salem. The pastor and his wife[1] reached out to us. They provided us a church and a home, a precious refuge from the competition of college and the constant fear of being sent to Vietnam.

This pastor could preach. When he preached, the power, the conviction and the tender mercy of the gospel made the human sanctuary resonate like Pavarotti getting overtones from the rafters. As I watched and listened, my conviction grew that what he did was what I had to do. I didn't know what it was that he did. I just knew that if what he did was what pastoral ministry was, I would be a pastor. What I was made to be was being jangled by what I saw him doing. One morning in church, as I watched him, I knew that I should be a pastor.

Walking down Winter Street, engrossed in thought, I surveyed my life's options. I liked history, and I knew that teaching history was something I could do and would probably enjoy. The prospect of pastoral ministry felt different. What this country Baptist preacher did qualitatively exceeded the bounds of human ability. What he did required God's Spirit. He wasn't a public speaker giving talks about religion; he was filled with the Holy Spirit and with the gospel of Jesus Christ.

I had two options. I could be a history teacher; I couldn't be a pastor. One was possible, the other was impossible. Since being a pastor was impossible, I decided to do that. I prayed: "Lord, being a pastor is impossible, so if you will be with me all the way to help me, I will be a pastor."

I figured that through and prayed that prayer in the time it took me to walk down the block to the mailbox to drop off a letter to my girlfriend in California. My covenant with God was signed, sealed and delivered by the Holy Spirit just as surely as my love letter was heading to California by U.S. mail. Both arrived and stuck. I became a pastor, and that woman became my wife.

That is the substance of my hearing of God's election and making covenant. I was following a trail God laid out for me. But not all was well. I had some serious misconceptions about God's call.

The Baptist pastor and I had become friends, so I resolved to announce to him (triumphantly) that I had decided to become a pastor. I phoned him, and we agreed to meet. I was expecting joyous approbation. What I received was lukewarm approval and a hint of sadness. I was confused at first, but later I understood.

If the church is a womb that saves and nourishes lonely and impoverished souls, I thought that being a pastor was climbing into the womb for good. I wanted the warmth and acceptance I received every Sunday. I wanted it all the time. Being a pastor seemed like the way to get it. He must have sensed it.

I misconstrued ministry as full-time security in the womb of the church. He knew that the call to pastoral ministry is a call out of the womb of the church into the perilous and painful role of being pregnant with the church, of giving birth to it, of nursing it and raising it.

Undergoing Preparation and Receiving a Call

After the hearing of election and making covenant, the next step is to undergo preparation. This involves formal education and rummaging around in the church doing this and that.

After one year in Salem I moved back to southern California and joined the staff of my home church, working twenty hours a week while I finished college. My responsibility was a group of about seventy-five junior-highers.

The first thing I did was to pitch the Sunday-school curriculum and write my own from scratch. I must have spent sixteen hours a week writing those lessons. I started at Genesis and worked my way through the whole Bible in two years. Each week I chose my text and spent hours and hours listening to every word of the text, over and over. Feeling my way through the text slowly, painfully, I tried to apply it to the junior-highers' lives. One at a time, each week, a lesson came. It worked; the kids learned and grew. And I learned and grew. I learned the value of spending the best hours of the week in the Word of God.

Seminary provides the privilege of studying great books and difficult ancient languages. Learning the ancient tongues of the holy text is of immense value. Seminary is all about learning to listen to different languages spoken by texts and people. If we can learn to listen to a text in Hebrew, we can learn to listen to a confused parishioner pour out his soul. The process is similar: both demand laying our syntax aside and listening for the image of God.

For field education I signed up for a supervised chaplaincy in a nursing home. That's how I met Daisy.

Daisy was a stroke victim in her eighties. She lived in a wheelchair. Daisy was aphasic; she couldn't talk straight. I couldn't understand a word she said, but her aphasia wasn't her problem, it was my problem. I had to figure out what she was saying.

I spent an hour each week listening to her repeat her words over and over. I couldn't be in a rush. Slowly her code emerged. With intense, painstaking concentration I could understand her and respond to her.

I deciphered that she was afraid to die because she was afraid of God. Each week she told me this in a different way. Each week in the conversation I came up with a new way to tell her that through faith in Christ she was OK with God. By the end of that year we understood each other. I could understand her speech, and she understood that God loved her. Her fear of God was gone, and so was my fear of other codes and syntaxes.

I struggled with Hebrew that whole year too. Initially those odd-looking letters and paradigms overwhelmed me as much as Daisy's mumblings. My paradigm needed to change. I needed to learn how to listen.

Preparation for pastoral ministry involves two things: learning to listen to the Bible and learning to listen to a human being. The skills aren't all that different. After all, both in their own way are the image of God. It's a matter of listening through many different codes and syntaxes for the image of God. It's always there. When we listen in love, we always find it.

The hearing and covenanting and preparation must be affirmed by a concrete call and ordination by an actual church, or there is no call. This is the one demonstrable, necessary requirement for knowing the call to pastoral ministry. It doesn't matter how called we feel or how much education we have: if no church will have us as its pastor, then we don't have a call from God to be pastor.

The people of God have a big hand in knowing our election as pastors. They're the ones who have to put up with us and our high-flying ideas about who we are. The church pays the bills. The church gains or loses from our ministry. So to the church God has entrusted a crucial step in the process. The church has to recognize the pastoral gift in us, the church must call us to serve, and the church must choose to ordain us. The church must lay hands on us.

During my seminary years the Baptist preacher moved from Salem to central California. His new church needed an assistant pastor at the time I graduated from seminary, so they called me to serve. They also proceeded with the process of having me ordained.

Bernard Ramm, a theologian, served on my ordination council. He didn't ask any theological questions, but his questions were the most theologically astute.

"Have you ever suffered?" he growled.

"Well, uh, yes, uh . . ."

My circuits raced to think of ways that I had experienced suffering in my life. He didn't expect much of an answer, and that is exactly what he got. He was making a statement: Pastors must be with suffering people, and they themselves must suffer. Pastors need to smell the bad breath of the cancer patient.[2]

On that issue, the issue of suffering, hangs the success or failure of the ministry. It is, in the final analysis, the issue at hand in call. God uses suffering to perfect his servants—even his own Son. In Hebrews we read about Jesus: "Although he was a son, he learned obedience from what he suffered" (Heb 5:8).

At issue is self-denial. Those who will suffer self-denial are parables of Jesus and are pastors. Those who will not are hirelings and thieves.

Discerning the veiled mystic call and enduring seminary studies is like following a faint, winding trail through deep darkness, seeking light. The light shines at ordination. The sermons, the robes and the charges are all prelude to the real thing about ordination, which is the laying on of hands. All ordained ministers present are asked to come forward and lay hands upon the ordinand.

The laying on of hands sets us in line with all those called, recognized and authorized by the church for thousands of years. Hands were laid on Paul and Barnabas. Jesus got a dove, David a flask of oil. It all means that this person is filled with the Holy Spirit to do ministry.

The Spirit of the Lord is on me,
　　because he has anointed me
　　to preach good news to the poor.
He has sent me to proclaim freedom for the prisoners
　　and recovery of sight for the blind,
to release the oppressed,
　　to proclaim the year of the Lord's favor. (Lk 4:18-19)

Knowing One's Self as a Pastor

Mystical experiences of hearing election and making covenant can be brought on by good intentions, stress or insecurity. Church work and seminary training don't screen enough. Bernard Ramm's warnings don't scare us off enough. Doing pastoral ministry is the final test of the call to be a pastor. Through experience we learn to know pastoral being; we need to find out what came out of the womb of God.

Pastors come in all personalities. Two older pastors I know and respect equally pastor their people in much the same way. One is introverted, reserved, bookish, a fine biblical scholar. The other is an extroverted, transparent crowd-lover who says cheerfully, "More books, more guilt." I'd love to have either as my pastor. For all their vast differences in personality, they both have a pastor's heart.

There are two parts to the pastor's heart: love for people and love for God.

Love for people must be differentiated from love of the experience of people. Some pastors love the experience of being around people. This is an excellent quality for a pastor (given the necessity of endless potlucks). Love of the experience of people is beneficial, but it is not a necessary personality characteristic. There are pitfalls for the pastor who loves the experience of people. It is easy to confuse loving being around people with actually loving people. The two are very different. Love of the experience of people is a form of self-gratification. Love of people requires compassion. The love for people that is absolutely necessary for the pastor is compassion.

The New Testament word for compassion is also the word for guts. The word is *splanchna*, from which we get our word *spleen*.

Splanchna is compassion for suffering and a love for people that goes physically deep. Jesus had *splanchna* for people. "Filled with compassion *[splanchna]*, Jesus reached out his hand and touched the man. 'I am willing,' he said. 'Be clean!' " (Mk 1:41).

Here is *splanchna:* When Jesus saw people suffering, his guts shook. This interior ache touched his will and moved him to action, a moral response. *Splanchna* is an interior, emotional reaction to an exterior phenomenon, but it is just as much a moral decision as it is an emotional effect.

I didn't know Bob—he wasn't connected with my church or any church—but I knew of his predicament. He was fifty years old, his abdomen was filled with cancer, and he was without hope. I usually don't do this kind of thing, but I called Bob up to see if he wanted a visit. He did.

He had been a tall, strapping postman, a weekend car mechanic. Now he was fed with a tube stuck into his chest cavity. His bowels had been ripped out in surgery. The conversation was labored; I don't know much about '56 Chevys. But we both were working hard at getting to know each other. I figured our first meeting was a total loss and this would be my last meeting with him. I asked him if he wanted a prayer. He did. I prayed short, but from my heart.

After the prayer I looked up. Bob was weeping, and so was his wife. My stomach flipflopped, my voice cracked. Not until then did I know that I would visit Bob until the end. Bob died a Christian.

For the pastor's heart, the love of God precedes love for people, exceeds love for people and guides the pastor in love for people. As P. T. Forsyth says, "The ideal minister must love and understand people, but must know and love still more the will and word of God."[3]

Love for God takes many forms. Thankfulness for God's many blessings, appreciation for the magnificence of God's creation and the intimate love of personal relationship with God through prayer are all important. One type of love for God surpasses all the rest. For the pastor, love for God takes on the particular form of love for the gospel of Jesus Christ. The gospel is the fact of God's salvation love for us expressed in the life, death and resurrection of Jesus Christ. The gospel preached, believed and lived is God's specific action of love toward us. There can be no separation between loving God and loving the gospel.

The gospel is the power of the love of God, and as such it gives the pastor the power of the love of God to give to others. If the gospel is the pastor's bread, the pastor will always have bread to give away.

God's love has a specific, concrete direction, to specific individuals, and we are called to love those people that God specifically calls us to love. The pastor is elect by God to do the actual work of pouring out God's electing love. This takes discretion and everyday sensitivity to the leading of the Holy Spirit.

Endurance

The fact that we are called by God to love a particular person does not mean that the recipient of love will like it. The specific, concrete love of God will often require us to love people who do not want our love in the way God requires us to offer it. The love of God to sinners through us, whatever else it may be, is always the gracious demand to repent. Even in the tenderest pastoral call on a gentle, faithful, persevering saint there is contained—implied if not stated—the quiet request to turn to God. The saint who is tender to God will always welcome it. It is no threat, it is sheer joy. But to the ill-tempered, the stubborn and the proud, all pastoral ministry, all pastoral love, will be a threat.

The call to repent assaults the Old Adam in us: the life of the flesh, our involvement in the sinful structures of this world, our stubborn refusal to yield to God's will. We cherish our sin, we clutch it, it kills us but we love it. The gospel demands that we choose life, rejecting sin and its ungodly demands. So the love of God in the gospel works like a surgeon. Cutting out sin's cancer, with pain like death, the gospel heals.

Most of us do not like the surgical role of the gospel. This is why we need God's specific definition of love to guide us in our work. Every time the parishioner winces ever so slightly, we want to stop pastoring. As Kierkegaard says, the pastor must "above all be able to put up with all the rudeness of the sick person without letting it upset him, any more than a physician allows himself to be disturbed by the curses and kicks of a patient during an operation."[4]

The ministry in all its parts—preaching, teaching, visitation, spiritual direction, church discipline, church politics—works under the Lord's sovereign hand to excise the pernicious tumor of sin from the parishioners we love. This process causes the Old Man to scream, bite, claw, threaten, slander and accuse.

Enduring this abuse is quite necessary. No pastor in his or her right mind likes it. Quite a few people, highly qualified for pastoral ministry in every other way, find this to be the point of impossibility for them. They must find other places to serve in Christ's kingdom. I still don't know whether I can take it. I take the problems one at a time as best I can. Enduring is never a triumph. It just happens.

Even for those who can somehow endure the kicks, it is a moral choice. Just as it is a moral choice to feel compassion, it is a moral choice to endure the kicks of the patient, to set one's face like flint (Is 50:7). Setting the face like flint is not the opposite of compassion. In Isaiah, it is the Servant of the Lord, the very one given "an instructed tongue, to know the word that sustains the weary" (50:4), who must set his face like flint.

The Cross of the Elect
Finally, in discussing the pastor's call to ministry we must creep up to the edge and peer into the abyss. We must explore the pastor's valley

of the shadow of death. We stare into the pastor, elect to be like God in the flesh: Jesus Christ the Godforsaken.

Discussions of God's election frequently gravitate to the issue of fairness. Is it fair for God to elect some and not others? Rarely in these discussions is real biblical election talked about. Rarely is it mentioned that election by God is always election for service. The true elect of God is always the servant of the Lord. As pastors we follow the One who in his service to God cried out,

My God, my God, why have you forsaken me?

Why are you so far from saving me,

so far from the words of my groaning? (Ps 22:1)

This is hard to talk about. But Godforsakenness is necessary to pastoral ministry. In our Godforsakenness we approach our closest likeness to Jesus Christ, the Parable of God.

To understand Godforsakenness we must rehearse briefly what has been said about call. Initially we hear God calling us to ministry, and we make covenant with him to follow the trail toward pastoral ministry. We undergo a process of preparation, sometimes rigorous and difficult. In it we learn to listen to Scripture, to listen to a person and to listen to God. At ordination the church formally recognizes our call and blesses us with the power of the Holy Spirit through the laying on of hands. We begin our ministry, and we encounter many things. We work hard and have some successes and some failures. We find through difficult experiences that we have been made for this work. Our hearts are filled with compassion for people, love for the gospel and endurance for the painful parts of the job. We feel God at work in us.

Then one day, for unknown reasons, God just isn't there anymore. The Presence that has guided and strengthened is gone. Our covenant with God feels broken and void. The Scriptures stop comforting. Every page condemns! We continue to read out of obedience, but the Word becomes the letter that kills.

Pastoral skills become worthless.

The church is no longer a warm, nurturing environment where friends gather. The church expels us from the secure womb. Evil rages against us. The boundaries of the church are not walls keeping evil out but a boxing ring keeping evil in, so that it can come back and strike us again and again and again. We can't run.

I'm up a tree. High, far out on a fragile limb I cling. I climbed out there because God said that he wanted me there and that he would be with me. Now the limb is cracking off the trunk. God isn't there anymore.

The picture changes like a dream. I am not out on a limb, but strapped to a tree. I am hanging from a tree. I am dying on a tree.

Pinched in God's vise, dangling helpless, I am made into the bait of God. But for whom?

Nobody pretty wants me now. The world wants winners. Nothing succeeds like success. Look good to attract the good-looking. Die to attract the dying. Suffer to know the being of suffering. Cry out to know Jesus' crying out. Hear the blood of the innocents screaming; searing pain rises from blood-soaked dirt.

Only now am I a parable of Jesus Christ.

III

The Holy Spirit

*And the Holy Spirit descended on him
in bodily form like a dove.
And a voice came from heaven:
"You are my Son, whom I love;
with you I am well pleased."*

LUKE 3:22

*G*od is filled with joy. The Father sends his delightful love to the Son, who in turn sends his delightful love to the Father in a never-ending interchange of joy within God. It is not a metaphor when in 1 John 4:8 the Scripture declares, "God is love."

The place of the Holy Spirit within God is not difficult to consider; on the contrary, thinking about the Holy Spirit of God presents us with a picture of great beauty. Using the simplest trinitarian concepts we can formulate the place and role of the Holy Spirit.

Consider the following sentence: "God the Father loves God the Son." There is a simple truth here. *God the Father* is the subject of the sentence, and *God the Son* is the object. *Love* is the verb. The Son is the object of the Father's eternal act of love.

Consider another sentence: "God the Son loves God the Father." We affirm the simple truth of this sentence as well—except now *God the Son* is the subject of the sentence, and *God the Father* is the object. *Love* is still the verb. In the first sentence we affirmed that the Father loves the Son; in this one we affirm that it is just as true that the Son loves the Father.

Where is the Holy Spirit? The Holy Spirit is the verb. The Holy Spirit is the love of God. There is nothing inside God but God—even the love of God within God is God. The love of God within God is the Holy Spirit. It is God's eternal will to give us this love, the Holy Spirit, and to make us laugh with joy as well. God's love is a surprise. As John says: "How great is the love the Father has lavished on us, that we should be called children of God! And that is what we are!" (1 Jn 3:1).

The verse rings with the surprise of joyous laughter. The love of the Father for us is incomprehensible; it makes us laugh. The Father sends his own love to us in the Holy Spirit. Through the Holy Spirit we enter into the love of God as his dear children. Just as the Father loves the Son and the Son loves the Father through the Holy Spirit, when we are given the Holy Spirit we participate in the actual love of God as his dear children. We share in the love of God as the Son shares in the love of the Father. The plan of God is for us to become like the Son, beloved sons and daughters of God.

Furthermore, it is God's will and desire that we glorify him, enjoy him and love him not as separate individuals but as a great collection, as a gloriously unified household in which God dwells. The Holy Spirit builds this building, the church, to be a place where God lives in love and from which the love of God goes out to the world.

It is this active, creative love of God that the pastor must be filled with every day, in every activity, for love is the power of God, the direction of God and the goal of God. Love is the work of God making the church.

Ministry without love is vanity. As Paul says, "If I speak in the tongues of men and of angels, but have not love, I am only a resounding gong or a clanging cymbal. If I have the gift of prophecy and can fathom all mysteries and all knowledge, and if I have a faith that can move mountains, but have not love, I am nothing" (1 Cor 13:1-2).

The Holy Spirit in Jesus' Ministry

Jesus was set apart for ministry by direct action of the Holy Spirit. With the alighting of the Dove at his baptism Jesus was set apart and filled with power for ministry. Jesus relied on the Holy Spirit throughout his ministry for direction and power. In describing his own ministry he declared that "the Spirit of the Lord is on me" (Lk 4:18).

The emblem of his sanctification for ministry, and the place where he received direction and power for ministry, was prayer. He escaped from his ministry with the crowds for periods of prayer, where he enjoyed loving fellowship with his Father through the Holy Spirit.

Jesus categorically denied that he could do ministry without direct communication with the Father. Furthermore, he described the direction and power he received from the Father for ministry as the love that the Father has for him: "I tell you the truth, the Son can do nothing by himself; he can do only what he sees his Father doing, because whatever the Father does the Son also does. For the Father loves the Son and shows him all he does" (Jn 5:19-20).

The love the Father gives to the Son led him throughout his ministry. This love is the Holy Spirit. The love of God is the direction and power of God in the ministry of Jesus and in ours as well.

We know that Jesus lived in sinless fellowship with God his Father; his anointing with the Holy Spirit was perfect in every respect. Nevertheless, Jesus sends his disciples out today to do his work anointed with the same Holy Spirit that led and empowered him. Jesus expects us to do the same things that he did, in the same way, with the same Holy Spirit. It is an amazing privilege, a joyous calling, to be filled with the Holy Spirit for ministry.

The Holy Spirit functions in the pastor's life as in Jesus' life. Because we are followers of Jesus Christ, the love of the Father is poured into our hearts. This love is the active, building power of the Holy Spirit. When we live our daily lives directed and empowered by the Holy Spirit, as Jesus was, we are like Jesus. Even though our ability to follow the Spirit's leading cannot come close to Jesus' ability, we are parables of Jesus Christ.

Filled with the Holy Spirit, we are chosen participants in the active, creative love of God. This is the sublime privilege of every Christian. It is the special privilege of pastors. We get paid a salary by our churches so that, being free of normal demands to make a living, we can spend our whole day participating in the intimate life of God.

The Holy Spirit Builds the Church

The Holy Spirit carries out the will of God to build the church. This is the objective truth of the pastoral ministry: the church is the work of the Holy Spirit.

The justification and sanctification of the individual members of the church are the work of the Holy Spirit. The union of all Christians around the world into the church, the communion of the saints, is the work of the Holy Spirit. The uniting and working of each individual church—building it up, inspiring its worship, sanctifying it, directing and empowering its mission—is the work of the Holy Spirit.

Since this is the case, all of the church's leaders, and pastors in particular, must be sanctified, directed and empowered by the Spirit to do the work of the Spirit, which is to build the church into the blessed household of God.

How can we talk about the Spirit's work of building the church from the perspective of the Trinity? A simple analogy from the construction trade may help. In the building of the church God the Father is the architect, God the Son is the plan and God the Holy Spirit is the contractor.

It is the will of God the Father to create the church in the image of his Son. The Son of God is the pattern for the church and for the individual lives of Christians. The work of the Holy Spirit is to implement the plan of God in making the church.

The plan of God for us is not hidden. It is right in front of us. We can read the plan: we are to be like Christ. We are to build a church that is the body of Christ, his presence on earth now. But simply knowing the plan is not enough. We need the coordination and the resources of the Spirit to build the church.

When a building is to be constructed, the contractor selects specific workers to do the job. Then the contractor directs each worker to his or her task, coordinating the building effort. Finally, the contractor supplies the workers with the building materials. Without the contractor, the workers are directionless and powerless. And when the workers do not follow the contractor's orders in construction, the building process has many delays. What is worse, the finished product may be dangerously flawed. With the contractor's direction and resources, however, the building process follows the plan, and the end result is a beautiful, functional, safe building.

It is the same with the Holy Spirit and the ministry. The Holy Spirit is the contractor of the church. The Holy Spirit sanctifies the workers; we are selected and set apart for the purpose of building the church. The Holy Spirit directs the workers; in our daily ministries the Holy Spirit directs our efforts. The Holy Spirit empowers the workers; for each task we face the Holy Spirit gives us the power we need. If on a daily basis we are set apart by the Spirit, directed by the Spirit and empowered by the Spirit, the church will be a beautiful building, the very household of God: a safe haven for needy souls and a joy to all who enter.

Set Apart by the Spirit

I live near a river. Fish live in it, and the willowy river bottom is home to mice and mountain lions. From my kitchen window I watch bald eagles, ospreys, golden eagles and hawks.

Eagles, ospreys and hawks ride the wind. It doesn't take much energy on their part. When geese fly they flap their wings, but birds of prey soar by catching currents.

They seek thermals. Columns of warm air rise from the earth filled with energy. The birds glide on the heated currents of air. A good thermal can lift them high into the sky without so much as a single flap of their wings. From their higher place they can see more ground and can fly longer and farther, and when the time comes to dive on their prey, they can plummet with great speed.

As I watch these birds, I think of pastoral ministry. I too seek thermals. My ministry isn't work, really. The Spirit lifts, gives vision, direction and power.

Pastoral ministry is not work. Pastoral ministry is riding on the free winds of the Spirit. It is catching winds that lift us to heights we cannot climb on our own. We can't stay in the air very long on our own strength, but we can seek thermals. Our soul-wings are made large that we might catch the Spirit.

Where are the thermals of the Spirit in our everyday lives? How can we catch the wind?

Just as the sun comes in the morning and warms land masses from which energy-filled thermals rise, the Spirit comes new every day and energizes spiritual masses. We must glide over these spiritual masses to catch the rising energy currents of the Spirit.

For me there is one spiritual mass I must fly over daily in order to catch the Spirit: morning prayer. My morning prayer isn't long. It takes about fifteen minutes. But it is a sacrament of my sanctification. I set aside a quarter of an hour at the beginning of each day in order to set the whole day apart for the Lord. In turn, the Spirit sets me apart for the work of the ministry and sets me on the right path for a day full of direction and power.

Dietrich Bonhoeffer describes the need for morning prayer and the supernatural difference both the exercise and the neglect of it makes:

The morning prayer determines the day. Squandered time of which we are ashamed, temptations to which we succumb, weaknesses and lack of discipline in our thoughts and in our conversation with other men, all have their origin most often in the neglect of morning prayer. Order and distribution of your time become more firm where they originate in prayer. Temptations which accompany the working day will be conquered on the basis of the morning breakthrough to God. Decisions demanded by work become easier and simpler where they are made not in fear of men but only in the sight of God. "Whatever your task, work heartily, as serving the Lord and not men" (Colossians 3:23). Even mechanical work is done in a more patient way if it arises from the recognition of God and his command. The powers to work take hold, therefore, at the place where we have prayed to God. He wants to give us today the power which we need for our work.[1]

Morning prayer is a fusion: prayer led by Bible reading, and Bible reading led by prayer. We pray the Scriptures, they pray in us and through us. The Scriptures inspire petition, confession, "groans too deep for words," personal reflection, praise, joy and deep confidence to face the rest of the day.

There are many possible schemes for morning prayer, but the only element necessary to all of them is psalm praying. The psalms call us to pray and teach us how to pray. They tell us what to pray for. In the strictest sense, praying the psalter is praying in the Spirit; what else could it be, since the psalms are prayers inspired by the Spirit? The psalter is a spiritual mass that we can count on to deliver the thermal power of the Spirit. One of my guides for psalm prayer is the psalter found in the Book of Common Prayer given me at my Episcopalian confirmation.

But I am not very good at morning prayer. First thing in the morning, morning prayer doesn't seem very important. Reading the sports page seems more important. Listening to the morning news seems more important. Anything can capture my attention when it's time for morning prayer. The propaganda on the box of cold cereal will do just fine.

I have a spiritual director whom I call upon to help me with my morning prayer. That is all we talk about. Without consistent spiritual direction I can't keep at morning prayer. With good help I can keep at it and enjoy it.

Neglect of morning prayer isn't caused by distractions. Distractibility is a symptom of a deep infection. The infection in me is my desire not to be set apart for ministry, not to be directed by the Spirit, not to be empowered to do ministry. It is, most specifically, my desire to swerve from the Way of the Cross, to set myself apart, to set my own agenda and to gather power from other sources. My refusal to do morning prayer is the Old Adam inside me, kicking against the sanctifying work of the Word and the Spirit.

Parishioners kick and scream against us as we minister Christ to them. Examining my experience of morning prayer instructs me in their dilemma. It is mine as well.

So I turn to the clock and don't refuse its truth, I force my eyes open. It's six in the morning; the family wakes soon. I've got to get going—shower for cleansing, cereal for calories, coffee for alertness. As I open the Scriptures, always beginning with a psalm, my heart is made alert to God through praise. Working through my simple Bible-reading schedule, I am prompted by the Scriptures to confess sin. The gospel reading fills me with power.

The morning routine of body care sets my body on course for a day of work. The morning routine of spirit care sets my spirit on course for a day of work. Without my shower, cereal and coffee, I stink, I'm weak, and I'm unalert. Without morning prayer my spirit stinks, my spirit is weak, and my spirit is unalert.

Clean water washes skin, Holy Spirit washes spirit. The day begins with the water and the Spirit. Out of the Holy Scriptures the Holy Spirit blows, lifting us to dizzying heights of power and vision. I begin the day filled with a fresh breath of the Spirit. I am ready to soar. I am set apart for the day's work.

Directed by the Spirit

I unlock the door to my office at 8:30 a.m., enter and turn on my computer. Besides my word processor and database, I have a program that helps me remember leadings of the Spirit. I put random, short items into it, and it sorts these items into lists of things to do and people to see. I can assign dates to the items, and the program will sort the items into schedules. One of the lists it makes is called "Today." My Today list forms every day from the items whose dates match today's date. On a typical Tuesday it may remind me that I have a council meeting to attend in the evening, that I have a letter to write, that I need to call someone about an administrative detail and that I have lunch with a parishioner scheduled at noon. My computer helps me to remember and sort these directions given by the Spirit.

The Holy Spirit directs every activity of the day. That many are rather mundane and scheduled does not take away from their quality as Spirit direction. Much of the Spirit's direction is everyday, ordinary stuff. A lot of it is just following through with a daily schedule and keeping up with commonsense pastoral responsibilities. When I hear that a parishioner is in the hospital, I don't agonizingly search the mind of the Spirit to see whether I should visit. I may need to pray for leading concerning when to visit and how to organize my schedule around a visit. But common sense tells me right away that I need to make the visit. Morning prayer is a matter of common sense. Sermon preparation throughout the week is a matter of common sense. Taking time off to pray is a matter of common sense. Taking time to read theology is a matter of common sense. Staff meetings are common sense. I know that I need to do these things, so I do not agonize over them. But neither do I trivialize them. These regularly scheduled, mundane events are the Spirit's leading, and carrying them out requires the power of the Spirit.

Very often the Holy Spirit leads us through our common sense. The pastor's common sense is the logical grid through which all decisions pass. This logical grid dissects whole questions into logical subquestions whose answers are to be found in separate categories of knowledge. These subcategories of knowledge include the pastor's life experiences, theology, Bible knowledge, psychological knowledge and the logic of love. Once the subquestions are answered, they can be integrated into a complete answer to the larger question. Sometimes this process is long and difficult, but most of the time it happens very quickly.

For example, sometimes I come into work Tuesday morning (I take Mondays off) and just don't feel like starting my sermon. I have to ask, Is it God's will for me to work on my sermon this particular morning? What makes sense? Is the stack of administrative work more important than my sermon preparation? Will I have adequate time later in the week to prepare properly? How do I work best? Doesn't my mind like to stew over things, so that the sooner I get started the deeper I can go in the Scripture and the better the sermon? My theology tells me that the sermon occupies the most important hour of the week and deserves to be started early in the week. But maybe someone is in particular distress and needs my special attention right away. The law of love may dictate a visit. Can I make the call later in the day? Is it better to visit in the afternoon? The ramifications go on and on. And yet common sense sorts out questions like these—often it sorts them out very, very quickly.

The pastor's common sense is crucial. Common sense speaks against laziness, rationalizations and procrastinations. Common sense is part of life; it is real knowledge gained in ordinary ways. We are the acting subject of our own common sense. But common sense has a transcendent quality. Common sense cannot be better than our best thinking, but it can transcend our lazy, shoddy thinking. When we are at our worst, our common sense can rise up, convict us of our sloth and set us on the right course.

Anyone who denies the Spirit's use of common sense in direction is not a mystic; that person is a gnostic. The gnostic hates creation and so despises knowledge that comes in normal ways. The gnostic seeks divine guidance through spiritual techniques that ignore the created order and normal thinking. The true mystic pastor loves creation and therefore loves God's ways of speaking to us through created means, including our common sense. For common sense is based on the love of creation. It comes from observation and experience in the world; it understands how things work because it loves the created order. People with common sense are inevitably people with love. It should not surprise us in the least if the Holy Spirit of love uses common sense to direct us.

Some issues are not so clear. I also have lists of impressions about people that I collect on Sunday morning and throughout the week. All Sunday morning I scribble things on my worship bulletin—things like

☐ "So and so looks weary; give them a call on Wednesday."

☐ "So and so are having trouble in their marriage; make a call soon."

I enter these impressions into my computer as well, and it sorts them into lists. As I look at the lists, I must determine which ones I need to act on right away. These situations require a different kind of direction from the Spirit, because it is not obvious from common sense how I should respond.

For instance, when someone is bitterly angry with me, sometimes I need to call on her or him right away. But sometimes angry parishioners need to be left alone for months, even years, before they are ready for reconciliation. It's hard to know when to visit right away and when to stay away.

Some pastors adopt a consistent style. Some pastors always confront angry parishioners; other pastors always avoid confrontation. These styles usually correspond to the pastor's personality. Some pastors like confrontation; others despise it.

Allowing personality to dictate pastoral ministry leads to imbalance and pastoral mistakes. It ignores the reality that when we are weakest,

God is strongest. And it ignores common sense. Common sense says that our personality's strengths, the solutions we gravitate toward by nature, will not always be the right ones. When it comes to these matters, pastors need divine guidance. Difficult decisions require long prayer, decision-making prayer.

Decision-making prayer is not an abandonment of common sense. Just the opposite: decision-making prayer consciously, deliberately, opens our process of common sense to the Lord. I think over each subquestion in the presence of God, asking for guidance throughout the process.

I begin with the simplest of prayers: "Lord, help me to make the right decision in this matter." Then I pray for the persons involved, asking for God's best for everyone. Then, slowly, I pray for each person, deliberately unwinding before the Lord everything I know about them. In prayer everything I know from the Scriptures that applies is brought to bear on the subject. Everything I know as a matter of psychological insight is thrown in. Every step of the logical grid of common sense is prayed through and prayed for.

This prayer takes time. The intensity of the prayer and the depth to which it goes usually correspond to the seriousness of the matter at hand. Prayer about whom to call on and when may be very short, just a minute or two. Prayer for guidance through a serious problem, on the other hand, may take hours, even whole days.

Normally prayer ends before there is an answer. I do not demand or even expect an answer right away. It is important not to rush to an answer, because the most important component of decision-making prayer is the prayer that the Spirit prays through me. This happens after my prayer is exhausted. It happens in the subconscious, sometimes for days at a time while I go about other activities. I notice tiredness. The Spirit's prayer creates inner stress and tiredness. The Spirit's prayer exacts a toll.

Answers come in many different ways. Sometimes they come with a flash of insight. Often the answer is suggested by a friend, a church leader, a spouse or a colleague. How the answer comes is not particularly important. The point is, because of my decision-making prayer, when the answer does come it makes sense to me.

That the answer makes sense does not eliminate faith. I must boldly accept the contingency of such answers. I may be hearing the whole thing wrong! I have heard things wrong plenty of times.

Seeking the Lord's guidance is always risk-taking. It is decision-making in which we stretch our thinking to the absolute limit and accept answers that suggest themselves in the most tenuous ways. This requires us to act in bold, leap-taking faith. The result of decision-making prayer is this: the leap makes sense.

Occasionally when I turn my computer on in the morning and survey the long list of things to do, I hear something in my spirit tell me to turn everything off, turn away from my normal tasks and listen to the Lord for special guidance. I simply have a feeling that there is something I should be doing that I am not aware of. I need to pay special attention to what it might be. The answer comes through prayer.

This kind of praying is different from decision-making prayer. In decision-making prayer, the issue stares me in the face. In prayer for special leading, the issue is that I don't know the issue.

My first step in this kind of prayer is to go over my schedule for the day to see whether a responsibility is scheduled that I want to avoid. I have had phony "special leadings" that arose out of my desire to shirk a loathsome task. When I detect mental trickery at work, I put the responsibility I wished to evade at the top of my list of things to do.

In decision-making prayer I usually leave my desk, find solitude and go over the issue bit by bit, deliberately bringing to mind and prayer everything I know about the issue. In special leading prayer, when I don't know what's coming, I sit tight. I wait for further instruction right where I am. And instead of surveying my mind on the matter, I attempt to clear my mind of all matters so that I can be open and yielding to the leading. This kind of prayer attempts to go from a vague suggestion to a specific task.

The leading comes in many ways. Sometimes, even though I had some calling planned, I stay in my office, read some theology and wait to see what happens. Often the phone rings with an urgent call, or someone drops in. At other times a picture or a name suggests itself to my mind.

I am rarely disappointed when I follow up on such Spirit-whispers. But I don't always hear things right, and I don't always obey things right.

I'd blocked out Friday afternoon for fishing; it had been a long week. Loading up the car, my arms wrestled with an ungainly load of waders, boots, rod cases and my fishing vest when the face of a particularly dear, elderly, infirm parishioner appeared on the screen of my mind. My spirit slumped. I knew she needed a call. But I wanted to fish. So I prayed for her and went fishing. She died. At the moment I received my little vision she was becoming ill. A few hours later she went into a coma. I could have seen her one last time.

Empowered by the Spirit

There is little to say about securing the power of the Holy Spirit. Once we are directed by the Spirit, the power comes as we do the task. In other areas of life in the Spirit it is different. We complement the Spirit's work of setting apart through our discipline of morning prayer. We participate in the direction of the Spirit through our thinking and praying in the Spirit. But for the power of the Spirit we simply go and do our task. The power comes in the doing.

A mother who sees her screaming child pinned under a burning car rushes over and lifts the wreckage off the child. She has no faith in her ability to lift a ton of steel. She has love that compels her to act. The power comes.

We can expect and must expect to wield the power of the Spirit. It is a sin for God's servants not to expect the power of the Spirit. Shirking responsibility because we do not expect God to act through us with the power of the Spirit is a great sin. The Bible calls it fear.

<u>Of all the sins of all God's servants recorded in the Bible, perhaps the one that angers God most is fear.</u>

God becomes furious with Moses for bickering with him about going to Pharaoh out of his fear.

Of the twelve spies commissioned by Moses to spy out the Promised Land, only two, Joshua and Caleb, believed that God would empower Israel to take the Land. The rest of the spies were afraid. They lacked faith and died in a plague. The people of Israel chose to believe the cowardly spies and were forced back out into the wilderness in order to die. Of that whole generation, only Joshua and Caleb, the two men who believed the Lord, entered the Promised Land.

During God's call, the young Jeremiah complained to the Lord about his inability. The Lord encouraged Jeremiah and warned him: "Do not say, 'I am only a child.' You must go to everyone I send you to and say whatever I command you. Do not be afraid of them, for I am with you and will rescue you, declares the LORD" (Jer 1:6-8). Later in the same discourse the Lord told Jeremiah: "Get yourself ready! Stand up and say to them whatever I command you. Do not be terrified by them, or I will terrify you before them" (1:17).

The solution to the problem of fear in the ministry should not surprise us in the least. The Holy Spirit of God—the active, present power of God—is the love of God given to us. And love drives out fear (1 Jn 4:18). To be released from fear, turn to love, listen to love, allow yourself to be moved by love.

Before I undertake a pastoral task that frightens me, I plead aggressively with God, reminding him to fill me with power for the sake of his love for the people. Like the importunate widow, I pound away at God in prayer, appealing relentlessly to his love. Following such bold, demanding, obtrusive prayer, fear becomes moot; love is in charge.

There are times when we feel a special unction of the Spirit. Sometimes during preaching, sometimes during prayer for the sick. Almost always during prayer for the dying. But most of the time, the Holy Spirit empowers our work transparently. We feel no power at all. Rather, we feel weakness, an inherent incompetence. This is because we *are* incompetent to be ministers of the gospel. It is implicit in the call to ministry: what we attempt is impossible. We are not competent to carry out the task of the gospel ministry. We are made competent by the Holy Spirit of God. Paul tells the Corinthians: "Not that we are competent in ourselves to claim anything for ourselves, but our competence comes from God. He has made us competent as ministers of a new covenant— not of the letter but of the Spirit; for the letter kills, but the Spirit gives life" (2 Cor 3:5-6).

But this competence does not feel like power at all. Paul reports power in preaching which feels like nothing but fear and trembling, yet it exhibits great power. It is the power of the cross. The cross is Paul's power:

> When I came to you, brothers, I did not come with eloquence or superior wisdom as I proclaimed to you the testimony about God. For I resolved to know nothing while I was with you except Jesus Christ and him crucified. I came to you in weakness and fear, and with much trembling. My message and my preaching were not with wise and persuasive words, but with a demonstration of the Spirit's power. (1 Cor 2:1-4)

The power of the Holy Spirit is the power to live in the Way of the Cross and become parables of Jesus Christ. How else can we define the power of the Spirit than as the power to be like Jesus? We may or may not feel the power of the Spirit, but it is always the power to live like Jesus, to do what Jesus did, to follow the road that Jesus walked: the Way of the Cross.

As parables of Jesus, we should not really expect to feel power at all. In a parable the item of comparison has no power and feels no power. The power is experienced by the recipient of the metaphor. In the case of pastoral ministry, the specific power experienced by the recipient of ministry is the power of the love of God.

The power of the Spirit has nothing to do with success in a worldly sense. The power of the Spirit is not the power to transcend our environment and act upon it as an unattached agent of power. The power of the Spirit is the power to condescend and subject ourselves to the weakness and suffering of the beloved. This is the secret of *splanchna,* the compassion of the servant of God for the people of God in suffering. Jesus always healed by drawing on the power of his compassion for the sufferer. No weakness, no suffering, no love, no power: it's as simple as that.

By 4:00 in the afternoon I am tired and ready to go home. I feel no power, only fatigue. I have an evening meeting, so I want to go home and rest.

Driving by the nursing home on the way, I think about seeing Sara. She is 105 years old and blind but full of visions of the Switzerland of her youth. Sara has never been to church during my tenure, and she never will until her funeral. But Sara is part of the church.

I've worked my shift, and I have the right to drive past her. I'm in no mood to face death. I try to imagine what I can say to help her. I'm afraid I have nothing to say to Sara. I am afraid of a 105-year-old invalid. But love says stop. She will die soon. She needs someone to stop and be with her. Common sense says stop, I haven't seen her for a while, and just a few minutes won't prevent dinner with my family.

When I get to her room, Sara is slumped in her chair, half conscious. I approach her, touch her hand and say, "Sara, it is Pastor Hansen."

She starts a bit, but shakes her head and comes to full consciousness. "Oh, Pastor Hansen, it is so good to see you today. How are things going for you, how is your family?"

She always wants to know how I am doing. I didn't feel a lot of love coming in; I *acted* on love. Now, in the midst of the conversation, I feel the love. It is powerful. It is the power of the Holy Spirit to work the ministry of the gospel in Sara's life. Throughout the conversation I follow love's lead, directing the conversation as my heart directs.

At one point she says, "Pastor Hansen, I am old, and I am ready to die. I want to die."

"Sara, it's OK, you're old enough to die. You've been around a long, long time, and the time when you will be glorified in the presence of Jesus Christ is very near. That will be a grand day for you."

She smiles and says without fear, but only with humility, "I hope so."

"Oh, yes, Sara. You will soon be with Jesus."

The visit ends with Bible reading and a prayer. I read the Twenty-third Psalm; she recites it by heart. I pray for her.

"Goodby, Sara. I will come and see you again soon."

"Oh, Pastor, please come again soon, and thank you so much for stopping by. Thank you so much for stopping by."

I walk away laughing, surprised at God's love. How did this come about? It was not my doing. God lavished his love upon us. Reluctantly, but following simple love, I became for a short time a parable of Jesus, and I did the work of Jesus. Sara felt it. I'd gladly do this job for free. The joy of God, which fills God, fills me. Life in the Holy Spirit is a life of joy.

IV

Temptation

Then Jesus was led by the Spirit into the desert
to be tempted by the devil.
After fasting forty days and forty nights,
he was hungry.

MATTHEW 4 : 1 - 2

Our plan was to hit the trail head at 6:00 in the morning, hike eight miles in to an alpine lake in the Bitterroot Selway Wilderness, fish the late morning and early afternoon, and hike out that afternoon, carrying plastic bags full of monster cutthroat trout with flesh as pink as salmon.

Six miles up, at seven thousand feet, it began to rain. We kept hiking. Frigid air screamed down the draw. We hid under a tree, but it was raining sideways, so we got soaked through our shorts and T-shirts.

My teeth started chattering, so we ate some snacks we'd brought along, thinking some calories would help. I reached down to unsnap my canteen from my belt, but I couldn't manage the simple task; my hands wouldn't work. "I can't feel them," I told my friend with a laugh. Fortunately, my friend, who was also beginning to shiver, realized that we were in trouble. He suggested we head home immediately. I stumbled behind him numbly. There would be no fish today.

I was in hypothermia, a deadly condition in which your body's temperature drops off a cliff. Once the tumbling begins, the body can't make up enough heat to break the fall. Unless an outside source of heat intervenes, you die.

After about two miles of hard hiking, I still wasn't warming up. But the wind died, the clouds broke, and a hot summer sun blasted us. We propped ourselves up against a south-facing hillside and let the sun warm us to the bones.

I have no idea how long we lay in the sun, but I remember what woke us. My friend glanced at the bush beside him and saw fat, purple Rocky Mountain huckleberries. The sun had plopped us down into a thicket about the size of a football field. For an hour and half we foraged that hillside like a couple of bears. We sauntered home warm and dry, stomachs and bags full of huckleberries. What sweet pies they made.

The Wilderness

In the wilderness we are unprotected. Our normal systems of shelter are not operative. Our walk through the wilderness is subject to the agenda of providence. This can be dangerous and delightful—often it is both. But the crucial feature of wilderness wandering is being out of control.

Unless we wrest control of our lives through religious hucksterism, the pastoral ministry is a pilgrimage through the wilderness. We go about our work unprotected, in a spiritual environment of great fishing, sweet thickets, storms and wild beasts, and we have little control over what we encounter when. As we walk we are subject to providence, and we are not in control. But we are tempted to rip our lives from the hands of God at every point.

It's easy to say that we want to follow Jesus in our ministry—until we hear Jesus tell us about the wilderness. Notice how he responded to another well-intentioned but ill-informed would-be follower: "Then a teacher of the law came to him and said, 'Teacher, I will follow you wherever you go.' Jesus replied, 'Foxes have holes and birds of the air have nests, but the Son of Man has no place to lay his head' " (Mt 8:19-20).

The thing that teaches us not to marshal our lives and tear them away from God is our appointed fast. In our fast we learn obedience and trust. We learn to trust each day, and each ministry opportunity, to God. We must learn to trust the Holy Spirit, and so we are led by the Spirit into the wilderness for our fast.

The Fast

The pastoral ministry is a fast, and it lasts our whole life. We squirm under the pressure of it, and we become vulnerable to temptation because of it. From it we learn to trust God, to obey God and never to quit. In our wilderness fast we become parables of Jesus.

The pastor's wilderness fast is to continue to live in the wilderness under its terms, to refuse to turn stones into bread. To live on what is provided, to partake gladly in what comes along, to allow the Lord to provide for all needs.

In other vocations men and women turn stones into bread. They apply their sweat and their talents to till the soil, to ply their trade, to sell their goods, to make their living and raise their families. From Genesis through Proverbs and into Jesus' parables we see the hard work of men and women trying to make a living, migrating when necessary, succeeding and failing, but with every encouragement to pray for their daily bread and then go out and work for it.

Pastors don't get to do this. We live on what providence provides in the wilderness. Our "fast" consists of eating what is provided. We do not apply our hands to the business of providing for our needs.

The exception of bivocational pastors does not disprove the rule. Paul, a bivocational missionary, considered his ministry the exception. He defended paying ministers as the norm. And even though he did raise his own income, Paul's call to ministry set the terms of where he worked. It was not the other way around. Laypeople minister where they find employment they can live on. Bivocational pastors and "tentmaking" missionaries find employment where they are called to minister and live on whatever they can make.

The pastor's fast is a necessity for ministry because it trains pastors in love. It teaches obedience through suffering, even as Jesus had to learn obedience through suffering. "Although he was a son, he learned obedience from what he suffered" (Heb 5:8-9).

In our society we have transformed the legitimate feeling of life-or-death need for "our daily bread" into a feeling of a life-or-death need for boats. We know that we don't need boats, but it *feels* like we need boats. The feeling that we need bread to survive is transferred to other things, so that procuring these things becomes a life-or-death issue. We expand the need to have bread into the need to have in general. We have become a people who must *have* in order to *be.*

Once we have the boat, it is inconsequential. We use it out of guilt. "I bought it; I'd better use it." Using the boat does not satisfy the desire that prompted the purchase of the boat. When our eyes were fixed on the boat unpurchased, the boat commended itself as the terminal solution to the ever-nagging longing to have. Once owned, the boat is superfluous. Some satisfaction was gained in the process of procuring it, but once the boat is had it is irrelevant. The essence of life today is not having—it is *having to have.*

The pastor's fast is designed to reshape (by force) someone who must have in order to be into a person who may have or may not have, because the pastor's being proceeds not from having but from the call of God to be love in all circumstances. Paul addresses us with surpassing clarity on this issue from his prison cell. He writes: "I have learned to be content whatever the circumstances. I know what it is to be in need, and I know what it is to have plenty. I have learned the secret of being content in any and every situation, whether well fed or hungry, whether living in plenty or in want. I can do everything through him who gives me strength" (Phil 4:11-13).

The pastor's fast forces us to learn that God provides us with all our daily bread so that we can be content in any and all circumstances and in no way have to take control of our own life and destiny. Of course this makes us feel as if we're going to die. We want to quit.

Wanting to Quit

The temptation to quit comes early.

The tempter came to him and said, "If you are the Son of God, tell these stones to become bread." (Mt 4:3)

We lust after a job in which we could turn stones into bread.

Pastors really do have the ability to turn stones into bread. Anyone smart enough to pastor a church successfully could pursue almost any career for better money and fewer hassles.

But it's not just money. I've never met an ex-pastor who didn't like his or her new job better. Some miss the profound privileges of the ministry, such as being with people at significant times in their lives. But they don't miss the privileges enough to return to the ministry. I've never met anyone who had left the ministry but was tempted to go back.

Meanwhile, almost every pastor I know is tempted to get out. Every pastor is tempted to break the fast and turn stones into bread.

I was exhausted from fighting against my wilderness circumstances. I was vulnerable at every point and not in control. One summer twilight my head lay in my wife's arms; I wept bitterly and told her I was quitting the ministry.

I began interviewing at the university to enter the Ph.D. program in psychology. I wanted, finally, to make a living. I studied for the GRE, not wanting to resign until my acceptance at the university was assured.

My shattered call lay in my conscience like a corpse on a battlefield. It stank the place up. Many of my expectations for ministry and many of my reasons for entering pastoral ministry had been proved to be foolishness and were offensive to me. I had a theology of the cross, but I despised myself when it was time for me to hang there.

Then, unaccountably, the clouds cleared. I did nothing to revive my call, but God's face shone upon me—partly through the love of friends who listened but did not judge, partly through the wise care of the area minister of my denomination, partly through a few books. Mostly, though, I can't explain it. The revival of my call was like lying in the sun and being warmed after being cold and wet. The wilderness of the ministry brought me both: the cold endangering storm and the warming, reviving sun. I lay there and was revived by the glory of the Lord. I felt called to preach from Jeremiah.

So I preached from Jeremiah that fall. I laughed with joy as I foraged the fire and brimstone of the weeping prophet. I gave up fighting with boards over money and my "rights," stopped fighting against life in the wilderness. I began to feed on the Word.

Jesus answered, "It is written: 'Man does not live on bread alone, but on every word that comes from the mouth of God.' " (Mt 4:4)

Ladder-Climbing

The Episcopal bishop was huge. His height and girth made the skinny lectern he stood behind look silly as he towered over us fifth-grade confirmands sitting in the front pew.

He addressed us with a warm smile, but we were not consoled. We knew what was coming. He was going to ask us questions from the catechism prior to giving us our confirmation blessing. He held the keys of the kingdom. We felt death hang over us. If we could not supply the correct answers, we knew our lives were over, in front of our parents, God and the world. This man had power. He was at the top.

During his comments preceding our examination, I came up with a mental diversion from my fear. As I watched him speak I imagined myself as a bishop. I felt the power, and I liked it. I'd be a better bishop than this guy. And my parents would be so proud of me.

I looked over at the young priest who had prepared us for confirmation. He beamed with pride. He was the bishop's son. That made me proud for him. All of us in the confirmation class loved him. He had worked carefully with us over every question, explaining the Christian faith to us with loving care. He'd made us feel as if our class was the most important event of his week.

I wanted to be like the parish priest. He had cared for us. I wanted to be like the bishop. He was at the top of the ladder.

The young priest never became a bishop. I heard twenty years later that he had left the parish ministry.

Our family changed denominations, went from priests and bishops to pastors and denominational executives. Our new denomination sponsored a huge high-school camp. Six hundred high-schoolers were there, all eager to wiggle free from parental supervision and experience the sixties, if only for a week. I had never been to summer camp before.

The main speaker at the camp had been a football star, and he now pastored a prominent church. He was a good speaker. I was disoriented in this new world. Here the pinnacle was not defined by office. I wondered how this man had gotten to be the main speaker. It did not occur to me that he was the main speaker because he was a football star and the pastor of a big, rich church. But it didn't take me long to catch on. This camp was crowded with ladders. The stratification was obvious even to a fifteen-year-old.

The camp director was a big shot, as was the main speaker. Then there were song leaders and activity directors. But the ladder-climbing was going on just beneath the camp leadership.

The counselors were college students, seminary students and assistant pastors. Some of the counselors were more important than others. Some addressed the camp with announcements. Some were in charge of games and small groups. What made it obvious was that the important counselors stuck together during free time and boisterously discussed church politics. The important counselors were assistant pastors and interns from the big churches. They seemed to be trying to get somewhere.

They spent very little of their free time with the kids.

My morning discussion leader was an unimportant counselor. Early in the week, on our walk from group discussion to lunch, he singled me out. He asked me if I had received Christ. I responded honestly that I had. Then he asked if I kept morning devotions. I shook my head in ignorance. I had never heard of such a thing. He invited me to join him for his morning devotions. We went to a small chapel, and he showed me a simple method of prayer and Bible reading. The power of the Spirit was there. That experience of the power of morning prayer never left me.

From that point on I felt a pull. I wanted to be like the important counselors, and I wanted to be like the counselor who had really cared for me. This created a problem. I knew that this man could never be an important counselor: he was black.

I wanted to be an important counselor, but I resented the system that excluded my friend.

By Thursday my contemplation of ecclesiastical ladders ended. I encountered something more captivating than the study of success—a romance bloomed with a beautiful girl. I made the right choice. Looking back, I know my preoccupation with her was healthier than my musings over the ladders in the body of Christ. At that camp my spirit blossomed, my hormones went into orbit, and I learned about ecclesiastical ladders. Since then I've seen what ladder-climbing does to the church.

Career Paths

I have no quarrel with the fact that there are big churches and little churches and that certain pastors have the requisite gifts and are called to pastor big churches and others have the gifts and calling to serve smaller ones. My high-school years and most of my college years were spent in a large church with a wonderful, humble pastor. The problem comes when we lust after the big, prestigious, strategic pulpits in the influential areas, disregarding what the Lord's will might be. It's idolatry. We need to hear what the Lord says to Baruch through Jeremiah: "Should you then seek great things for yourself? Seek them not" (Jer 45:5).

Most of us reject the idea of ladder-climbing. But pursuing a particular "career path" as a religious professional is nothing more than a euphemism for ladder-climbing. It doesn't take long to figure out how to do it.

Just choose the right denomination with plenty of ladders to high places with good money, go to the right seminary, get the right internship in the right churches, begin with the right assistantship in the right church in the right area, flatter the denominational officials, get appointed to the right committees, get seen in the right places, get the right recommendations and send your résumé off to the right churches in the right areas. Ladder-climbing doesn't end when the right position is reached; it accelerates. Many ladder-climbers justify their ambition-driven climb by telling themselves that they will stop being ambitious and really serve the Lord once they reach their goal. But that doesn't happen. The climb goes on and on. No matter how big the church they serve, they believe it needs to grow. If the television ministry reaches half a million viewers, it needs to reach a million. If the sanctuary holds a thousand, a new one must be built that holds two thousand.

Ladder-climbing pastors destroy their families. They organize their family life around their career. As they consider a move to find a better position, they are only superficially concerned whether the timing is God's, let alone what it means to their family. Spouse and children are left alone night after night as they pay the price for the pastor's stardom. But the worst thing is when it dawns on them that their pastor/parent is a power-hungry religious professional and not a devoted servant of Jesus. Their faith shrivels.

Sometimes I wonder if ladder-climbers ruin their family's lives or if pastors who have lousy family lives become ladder-climbers. Ladder-climbers can't love; they can only use the people in their life. So pastors who have a hard time with love turn to ladder-climbing, because ladder-climbing is always easier than love.

Ladder-climbers destroy churches. There is a crisis in the small churches in our country. Many of these churches are weak, ingrown and damaged. Many do not trust pastors. They have never known a pastor's love; they have only known a pastor's lust. They have been simply rungs on the climb to success. These churches are so accustomed to being used by pastors that they never learn how to love a pastor. They have been courted and jilted time and time again. They learn not to trust. They punish pastors. Pastors willing to engage small churches in long-term, substantial ministry can teach these churches to love and trust pastors again, but it's hard work.

Ladder-climbing pastors destroy large churches. Once they get to the top, they can't switch gears. They got to the top by being good at ladder-climbing, and that's all they really know how to do. They do not know how to pastor. These churches rot from within. Staff members of these churches suffer enormously. The big church model these days is that the senior pastor cares for the church staff and the staff then cares for the people in their program areas. This theory breaks down if the senior pastor rose to that position through ladder-climbing. These "pastors" cannot pastor. They only know how to use people. So their staff members, who are pouring their lives into the people they serve, are not pastored. They are only pushed to work harder and harder, to make the church continue to grow so the senior pastor can continue to climb the ladder through their work.

There is an exception to this scenario, when the staff member is a ladder-climber as well. Opportunists thrive under a ladder-climbing senior pastor, because they understand intuitively the motivations of the ladder-climbing system. They *want* the senior pastor to push them for more work and more numbers. They want to be seen as producers. Since they have a hard time with love, they don't want the senior pastor's love and support. And frankly, because many of them have a difficult time with intimacy at home, they want to be asked to be out night after night on the holy crusade.

Ladder-climbing staff members are ideal colleagues for ladder-climbing senior pastors, except for one thing: ladder-climbing staff members will use the senior pastor, just as the senior pastor uses people. They will listen to gossip about the senior pastor, and they will spread it. They relish the flattery of disgruntled parishioners who are using them to attack the pastor. These staff members will split the church if they believe it will benefit them.

Making the Choice

There is no other possible conclusion: every pastor must choose between ladder-climbing and love. I've tried and tried, but I've never been able to mix ambition and love. When I'm trying to be important and I'm plotting my way to the top, I can't love my wife, I can't love my kids, I can't love my friends, I can't love my parishioners. When I'm climbing ladders I cut myself off from the power of the pastoral ministry, which is love. For me to love, for me to follow Jesus, I need to step off the ladder.

And yet in my flesh I am a ladder-climber. I saw it young, and I identified with it young. I learned it young. I have caught myself ladder-climbing again and again. I have hurt people with it.

Nevertheless, in my spirit I am a pastor. I also was pastored well at a young age. I also learned that young. I identified early on with men and women who cared for me in the name of Jesus Christ. I have been a pastor to people, and I know the power of love.

What a divided person I am! Raised in the church, I am heir to its life and heir to its damnation.

I accept these truths about the pastoral ministry and about myself:

1. I have to choose between ladder-climbing and love.
2. I have in me the desire to climb ladders and to love.

3. I must live in constant repentance for my desire to climb ladders and in constant turning toward the God of love.

The real nub of the temptation to climb ladders is the lie, fed me by the devil, that I can climb the ladder and love those around me at the same time. It centers on me. It feeds my ego. I think that I can be the unique individual who can plot a career and serve the Savior. I am strong enough to handle the disparity.

Ladder-climbing begins with as trifling a thing as a daydream.

> The devil took him to a very high mountain and showed him all the kingdoms of the world and their splendor. (Mt 4:8)

It proceeds to a lie. We imagine that we can temporarily leave love and the Way of the Cross for a slight and momentary detour on the ladder. It need be only for a moment. Then, we tell ourselves, we will return to our life of love, only in a better setting, a bigger pulpit, a better salary, with more prestige. Just climb the ladder a little while; then we can take the time to love. All it takes is a bow of the head.

> "All this I will give you," he said, "if you will bow down and worship me." (Mt 4:9)

Pandering

We pimp shortcuts. Everybody wants them. People will pay good money for them. We love cheap love and hate the costly cross. By giving people shortcuts we are cheating them out of life in Christ, and it destroys us. Entertainment, management and counseling[1] are valid activities in their proper arenas, but for pastoral ministry they are easy outs, quick fixes, short-term satisfaction, shortcuts that bypass the cross.

One symptom that shows us we are making shortcuts for our people is being too busy. For instance, I could fill up many hours every day with counseling. People believe counseling is a great panacea. Yet many are loath to go to a professional counselor. That costs money, and real counselors ask hard questions.

What I do is a mixture of personal friendship, spiritual direction and discipleship. I go where people are—yes, I make house calls—visit with them and listen to them. They like that part. But when it comes to the solution part of my dialogue, they find out that I get real moralistic and even pretty demanding. I tell them what Jesus says about their situation and that they need to repent of their sins and start following him.

Of course I am sensitive to men and women who have been subjected to severe mental and physical abuse. Their shattered souls soak up guilt the way acoustical tiles absorb sound. I have referred many such people to competent counselors and continued my pastoral care. But many of the people who come to me for counseling want a quick fix; they want me to give them a way around living a moral life, a shortcut to happiness that skips following Jesus in costly discipleship.

In our hypertherapeutic milieu, people want professionals to do something to them to make them feel better. Living through life, meeting the demands of following Jesus, living under the lordship of a holy God doesn't appeal to the general public these days. The majority of Americans will tell any pollster that they believe in the Ten Commandments. But only a small percentage of those people could even recite the Ten Commandments, and an even smaller percentage have any genuine interest in following them.

For me, trying to be a counselor is a shortcut. It is pandering to my people's desires to have me do something to them rather than admonish them to live through the thick forests of their lives by following Christ in discipleship.

Since I do discipleship instead of counseling, I find I have a fair amount of free time on my hands, time I can spend praying.

I've never heard a pastor tell me he or she was too busy praying to do other things. I've only heard pastors say they were too busy doing things like counseling, organizing worship extravaganzas and managing church affairs to spend much time in prayer. Need we inquire further why the devil wants us busy, pandering to our people's desires for shortcuts?

There are other shortcuts our people want from us. For instance, people need to worship God, but they want to be entertained instead. Maintaining worship as a vertical dialogue with God in which we eschew entertainment and press our minds and bodies into service is a battle against one of the public's deepest felt needs.

Boredom is so extreme in our day that people feel they are dying. Boredom makes people feel as if their central nervous system is winding down and shutting off. People will pay any amount of money to relieve boredom for the same reason that they will pay any amount of money for a pacemaker.

People want singing that excites and envelops, special music that impresses, sermons that warm the heart, testimonies that make them cry and miracles that make their skin tingle.

Worship as entertainment, defined as the ritual excitement of the central nervous system to temporarily relieve boredom, is a shortcut to the believer's soul-deep satisfaction of serving God through vertically oriented worship. Entertainment is passive and is an effect wrought upon the participant by the "worship leaders." Worship is active and requires effort expended by a thankful congregation of believers on behalf of a holy and merciful God, initiated and led by the Holy Spirit.

If we entertain people, our church will grow. If we lead in worship, our church may shrink until it is composed of a group of people who want to worship. Then the church has a chance to grow based on the precedent of worship. The church that worships will have many visitors who never come back, and a few who cannot stay away.

Perhaps the most common shortcut people want from their pastors comes from the fact that people need leadership, but they want to be managed instead. Most pastors think management is leadership. But the people know the difference. People don't want to be led; they want to be managed.

A leader lives with the church through every ugly bit of its corporate life, whereas the chief concern of management is to avoid every ugly bit of its corporate life. The strategy of management as ministry is to avoid the pitfalls of the corporate life of the church by abstracting the pitfalls and following a program to avoid them. But in the Christian life we are not meant to avoid pitfalls; we are meant to live our lives *through* the pitfalls as the actual stuff of life in Christ.

The difference between management and leadership can be summed up in a single sentence: *People don't want to be led through the valley of the shadow of death; they want the valley of the shadow of death to be managed for them.*

Trying to be a manager, the pastor analyzes the church as a human system, using scientific principles of human-resource management. The pastor translates the analysis of the system into an abstract equation of the human resources of the church. This analysis includes the church's strengths and its weaknesses, the goals the church understands as its mission, the obstacles hindering the church in reaching its mission, and a program that is a plan of action by which the church can maximize its strengths, minimize its weaknesses, overcome its obstacles and achieve its mission.

For management, the weaknesses and obstacles facing the church are never the sins of the church. In the management model, churches don't have sins. Rather, the church is the victim of the chaotic world it lives in. The church's weaknesses and obstacles come from living in this world. Therefore the purpose of programs is to enlighten the church to the methods by which it can transcend the morass of this world. The pinnacle of insight is the program.

The next step for the pastor attempting to be a manager is to teach the program to the church. In this stage the pastor must attempt to execute control over the individual members of the group by "selling" them on the program with slick promo material, posters and small group discussion. Members must give up their will—not to the mission of the church, not to the Lord of the church, certainly not to any kind of repentance and not even really to any kind of action: they must simply make a firm commitment to the viability of the program as an article of faith.

After many years of trying to sell programs to churches and watching others attempt the same, I am convinced that once the members of the group believe in the program, the process is over. For all intents and purposes, church members are perfectly satisfied with the results of management if they can simply come to believe that a program exists which will deliver them from their problems and usher in a new era of fulfilling the mission of the church. I don't think that anyone really wants to follow the programs. People just want to believe in programs. This is why pastors and laypeople love going to seminars and convocations so much. They really have no serious intention of implementing anything they learn. They just want to experience learning about a new program.

Otherwise how can it be that our churches are analyzed over and over, we are presented with program after program, none of which works, and yet we want more and more programs? The fact is, no one expects these programs to work. We simply want to experience believing that they work, so that we can live our lives together without risking a thing, without repenting of a single sin.

Making shortcuts for our people makes us feel important. Counseling, entertaining and managing are three activities our society values as relevant. We think we are making our ministry relevant to people's needs. But when we make our ministry relevant, we lose what is material to the ministry.

We do have allies in the church. Many of our people don't want us to lose what is material to the ministry. The ruling boards of three churches I have served all breathed long, loud sighs of relief when I told them that I don't believe in church growth programs. They'd already seen how destructive they can be. When I've pastored churches that thought entertainment was worship, people have been happy for me to slowly but surely restore dignity and enhance the verticality of worship.

I'll never forget sitting at a lunch table next to two well-seasoned denominational officials while they discussed their problems placing pastors in churches. I overheard one say to the other: "I'll trade you ten pastors who counsel for one that can preach."

"No, I won't trade you," the other responded. "When I find one who can preach, I never let go of them."

The soul of the church is being lost to a pandering pastorate. The church needs pastors who lead the church in repentance with love. The church needs pastoral leadership that refuses to take the shortcuts and has the courage to allow the church to suffer so that the whole church can be a parable of Jesus. This is what is lost when pastors deliver shortcuts. When the pastor takes the church off the Way of the Cross, the church stops being the parable of Jesus, the body of Christ.

> The devil led him to Jerusalem and had him stand on the highest point of the temple. "If you are the Son of God," he said, "throw yourself down from here." (Lk 4:9)

We think we pander to people because we are insecure. We flatter ourselves with our psychological shortcomings. We excuse our sins by saying we have a need to be liked. But pandering is not a psychological problem. Pandering is a moral problem. We pander to people's desires for shortcuts because we don't want to walk the Way of the Cross with them. We want shortcuts just as much as our people do.

Jesus was tempted by the devil to jump off the top of the temple and excite the people. The devil tempted Jesus to become an instant messiah. He tempted Jesus to leave the Way of the Cross, to pander to the people, to give them a shortcut to glory.

The devil told Jesus to jump, assuring him that surely God would save him. Jesus replied: "It is also written: 'Do not put the Lord your God to the test' " (Mt 4:7).

Jesus knew what would happen if he left the Way of the Cross for the cheap shortcut. If he jumped off the temple, he would crash on the cobblestones below. The devil is a liar.

V

Eschatology

I tell you, my friends, do not be afraid of those
who kill the body and after that can do no more.
But I will show you whom you should fear:
Fear him who, after the killing of the body,
has power to throw you into hell.

LUKE 12 : 4 - 5

*E*schatology is a big word with a simple definition. Eschatology is the study of the world's end. It is the study of Christ's return, the millennium, the tribulation, the judgment before the great white throne, the new heaven and the new earth. In this chapter I will discuss only one small branch of the great tree of eschatology, the doctrine of hell.

Eschatology is not only about the world's end, it is about our personal end as well. It is about where we go after we die. It is about heaven and hell. Much of what is associated with eschatology, such as the doctrine of the millennium, seems at best distantly relevant to our personal lives. But each of us knows that we can die at any time. The day we die is the Day of the Lord for us. And we want to know what that day will bring.

As pastors, we have a responsibility to teach people where they go when they die. They want to know. They have a right to know, because the Bible has extensive teachings on the subject of heaven and hell. If we can't teach our people where they go when they die because we don't know ourselves, or if we feel that we cannot teach them what we really believe about heaven and hell, we are poor pastors.

I have at times fit my own definition of a poor pastor in this regard. I won't excuse myself. But I've struggled deeply with the doctrine of hell. I think this doctrine is hard to understand and difficult to believe.

There is an important place in the ministry for honest questioning over doctrinal issues. But I'm not proud of my tossing and turning over hell. Some pastors wear their agnosticism about hell as a badge of honor. I've tried it. I've acted as if struggling to believe our Lord's words were a virtue. But I always found that when I became proud of my doubts, they suddenly became the sin of unbelief. For me, finally, waffling over hell became the sin of unbelief.

To say that I've struggled with hell is to say that it is a part of my story as a pastor. In fact, every pastor's story is in some sense an intellectual history. This part of the story is as vivid to me, as emotionally intense, as any crisis in my life. The stakes were as high, because having a coherent, biblical eschatology is absolutely vital to all pastoral ministry, and especially to preaching.

Eschatology was certainly the vital presupposition of the first disciples. They went out into the Roman world with the Spirit of God and an eschatology. It was the Spirit of Jesus and it was Jesus' eschatology. It was the eschatology he had taught them during his ministry, augmented by what they had learned through his death and resurrection. Their sermons were eschatology. They preached the crucified and risen Son of God, whose life, death and resurrection were the beginning of the end of the world. It was preaching with consequences, preaching with power.

Too many of us fancy ourselves big on the Spirit and are proud that we know little about eschatology. Yet if we preach less powerfully than the early disciples, if we preach less powerfully than preachers just a generation ago, it might be because we lack their ammunition. The widespread lack of a coherent, biblical eschatology among mainline denominational preachers is largely responsible for the flaccid, sentimental preaching that is emptying our churches.

My history with hell began early. It began with the process by which I was saved from it.

Saved

In fifth grade my Episcopal Sunday-school teacher told our class that if each of us was baptized, was confirmed and had received Communion, we were saved from hell. That sounded good to me. It meant I was on a fast lane to heaven. I did have a question though.

I asked her about children who died without being baptized, confirmed or receiving Communion. She told us that baptism was the important thing. Then I asked her, What if an unbaptized child was in an automobile accident, was lying in the street and had just a few minutes to live, and there was no priest to baptize the child—what then?

The teacher, who had been extremely patient up to this point, remained so. She calmly told me that should I ever encounter such a circumstance, I should baptize the child myself, as it lay in the street taking its last breaths.

An image came to my mind; I held on to it for a moment and then blurted it out. I asked her, "What if all I had was a full bucket of water—should I pour the whole bucket on the child?" I was hoping for a comic response, and that was what I got. The class busted up, her patience evaporated, she changed the subject. And I eventually became a Baptist.

My sacramental security grounded me until I met a kid in high school who invited me to my first-ever crusade.

It was a theater in the round. The audience sat in darkness, but the stage was brightly lit. The service began with singing that I thought was real dorky. Then the Christian weight lifters came on. It was a carnival. This didn't look like Holy Eucharist, and when the preacher jumped on stage, he didn't look like a priest.

He preached hot as hell. I'd never heard a salvation message before, not even a gentle one. All the priest's homilies I'd heard assumed that we all were saved—after all, all of us took Communion. This guy divided us up. He said that some of us had never received Christ before and were going to hell. After a while I figured out I was in the group he thought was going to hell. I accepted Christ that night, though I didn't walk forward. "I walk forward every Sunday," I thought.

My ecumenical experience expanded when our family joined a Presbyterian church. The Presbyterian pastor, like the hellfire preacher, didn't assume that everyone he preached to was saved. He preached strongly evangelistic sermons about being saved from hell, without the hellfire style. I wanted to emulate his thought-provoking style. At his church, during my high-school years, I began to care about evangelism.

I wanted people to be saved from hell. I began to tell my friends at school about Christ. Some friends and I put together a Jesus band and we traveled around, singing and testifying to the power of Jesus to save. I believed implicitly in hell.

Though I was a Presbyterian, I was what theologians call an Arminian. I believed that everyone had to make their own free-will choice to receive or reject Christ. But I was beginning to run into Calvinism in corners of the Presbyterian church. Calvinism teaches predestination, the idea that God chooses those who go to heaven. The idea repulsed me. I couldn't square it with hell. Hell, I thought, had to be someone's choice. At the time I couldn't believe in Calvinism *and* hell, so I chose hell.

The usual questions that dog young people about hell didn't bother me. I didn't worry about the destiny of babies who died (even ones who weren't baptized); I knew that God is merciful. I never believed that hell could be flames and worms. I picked up a vague sense that hell must be spiritual pain.

Why Not?

My first semester of seminary I decided to take on Martin Luther. I researched the Luther-Erasmus debate on the freedom of the will. I read Erasmus and was thrilled with his winsome defense of the freedom of the human will to accept or reject God. Turning to Luther, I felt certain he would lose this theological Super Bowl.

One by one, Luther bludgeoned Erasmus's arguments. As Luther persevered thickly, my perseverance thinned. My grip on Arminianism loosened. My grip on my inner life loosened. A transformation took place, a kind of theological conversion actually. As I let go of my belief in the power of my will, my life refastened itself on the graciousness of God's will. My eyes moistened and my guts rumbled as I recognized that my life was not an accident of human will and circumstance, but the result of the active love of God. I already believed this about my call to ministry. I knew I had been chosen for ministry. Now I knew I had been chosen for Christ.

As soon as I finished *Bondage of the Will,* I purchased Calvin's *Institutes of the Christian Religion* and devoured it.

My newfound Calvinism threw a wrench into my doctrine of eternal punishment. Here before me was the ultimate horror: God choosing people to go to hell. I loved Calvinism but could not tolerate its dark side. I would not give up on Calvinism, so hell suffered in the balance.

I ran into annihilationism. This teaches that there is no eternal hell; nonbelievers are simply annihilated at the last judgment. Annihilationism manages to steer clear of universalism and the offense of eternal hell. It lightens the burden on Calvinism, since souls not chosen do not suffer forever, they simply cease to exist.

I embraced annihilationism wholeheartedly. But I couldn't preach it. I accepted a call to a Baptist church where everybody believed in the existence of hell. I tried to explain my view to some people, but they got lost in my arguments. Annihilationism sounds logical; it is built on some points of biblical anthropology. But the big problem with annihilationism is that it isn't really in the Bible. You can deduce it from some Bible texts, but it isn't in plain sight. Biblically, universalism stands on steadier ground than annihilationism.

I began to look at passages in Romans that tended toward universalism. I paid attention to the *alls* like those in Romans 5:18-19: "Consequently, just as the result of one trespass was condemnation for *all* men, so also the result of one act of righteousness was justification that brings life for *all* men. For just as through the disobedience of the one man *the many* were made sinners, so also through the obedience of the one man *the many* will be made righteous." And Romans 11:32: "For God has bound *all* men over to disobedience so that he may have mercy on them *all.*"

Those are some pretty serious *alls.* Many highly respected commentators hint that these passages mean that Paul taught universal salvation—commentators like C. K. Barrett, Ernst Käsemann and of course Karl Barth.[1] Barth comments on Romans 5:18-19 as follows: "In the light of this act of obedience there is no man that is not in Christ. All are renewed and clothed in righteousness, and all are become a new subject, and are therefore set at liberty and placed under the affirmation of God."[2]

Universalism cast a spell on me. It was like puppy love; I could think of nothing else. Everything was right in the world at last. Universalism and Calvinism work very well together (as long as we don't take Calvin too seriously). In this view God chooses certain ones to be Christians, who then are the kingdom of God in advance of everyone else's eventual discovery that they belong too.

E. P. Sanders, however, was not nearly so concerned to make Paul look like a universalist. In his *Paul and Palestinian Judaism* Sanders cites the many times in Paul's letters that he talks about those that will be destroyed on the Day of the Lord: 1 Corinthians 1:18; 2 Corinthians 2:15; 4:3; Philippians 3:19. Commenting on the *alls* of Romans 5:18-19, Sanders says:

What he actually thought is abundantly clear in passage after passage: apart from Christ, everyone will be destroyed; those who believe and participate in the body of Christ will be saved. Thus he means really neither "all . . . all" nor "many . . . many," but "all . . . many." . . . The real force of the analogy is given in Romans 5:17: if one man's trespass led to death, *all the more* will those who accept it receive life through Jesus Christ.[3]

When I read Sanders I was in no mood to hear that a universalist exegesis of Paul might be wishful thinking. I tried to ignore it, but Sanders's no-nonsense approach to Paul stuck in my mind.

Barth is famous for denying throughout his life that he was a universalist. He knew that universalism is patently unscriptural. In his doctrine of predestination, however, he radically reinterprets the traditional Reformed doctrine of the predestination of individuals into the predestination of the One Man, Jesus Christ. For Barth, Jesus is the Elect Man. All persons are elect in him. This throws the possibility of universalism wide open. Although Barth denied being a universalist, in response to questions about the possibility of universal salvation he consistently replied: "Why not?"[4] Barth's happy "Why not?" metamorphosed in my mind to "Absolutely yes!"

I began to see people in a different light. I began to see everyone around me as heavenbound. It felt good. It gave me a happy feeling. (That should have been a warning sign: my generation of theologians loves to believe doctrines that make us feel happy.)

What was unhappy was that I was a secret universalist. I preached sermons hinting at the possibility of universalism, but I was too insecure, too unsure of my new theological view, to share it widely. Pastors don't talk about it. I knew pastors with universalist ideas, but very few would talk openly about it; most were afraid to admit it. That confused me. Here's this happy doctrine—everyone gains eternal salvation—but almost no one will talk about it. Why not? I couldn't answer that question. All I knew was that *I* didn't want to talk about it.

Universalism relieved some of my theological tensions, but it made my ministry frivolous, pointless. I discovered firsthand in my pastoral work what J. S. Whale said about universalism in his book *Christian Doctrine:*

> It is illogical to tell men that they must do the will of God and accept his gospel of grace, if you also tell them that the obligation has no eternal significance, and that nothing ultimately depends upon it. The curious modern heresy that everything is bound to come out right in the end is so frivolous I will not insult you by refuting it.[5]

My faith devolved into a mild pantheistic pluralism, and I began to despise it. It was paltry, toothless. With the major paradoxes, like the doctrine of hell, taken out, my faith was as flabby as a week-old helium balloon. My ministry became futile and pathetic; I was of no use to anyone.

Something happened I never expected. My anger toward my parishioners increased. I would have thought that dethroning the "angry" God of the Bible would have made me into a kinder, gentler pastor. Just the opposite actually occurred. I became more resentful of people who hurt me. Pastors are like football quarterbacks: they need to be able to take a hard shot from their opponent and get up smiling. But I lost my durability. I got prickly over the normal bumps and bruises of pastoral work.

These bumps and bruises come most of the time from Christians. I didn't think that because they were bumping heads with me they should go to hell. It's just that there's something about eliminating the God of judgment that makes us into judges. When I gave up on a God of vindication, I became my own self-appointed vigilante.

The area of ministry that my new eschatology affected most was my preaching. At first it didn't change much. I tried to continue preaching Christocentrically. But I became more and more interested in preaching psychological insights. It didn't occur to me that I was becoming a syncretist. Yet slowly I edged Christ out of my preaching. I stopped preaching evangelistically and began to offer "relevant" social and psychological interpretations of the Scripture. The only reaction I got, even from my liberal listeners, was that my preaching was getting boring.

I suppose for me, the most important minutes of sermon preparation are the ten to twenty-odd minutes I spend during the worship service gazing out over the congregation during the offering, the choir number, and the announcements. I look out to see who's there and who isn't. But I'm not taking roll, I'm taking stock. I look into eyes. I look into lives, I look for needs. I look for hard hearts that need to be softened and for tender hearts that need to be encouraged.

What I see at first is a crowd, a public gathering. What I'm looking for is an assembly of people made in the image of God, called by the Holy Spirit this very morning to hear the holy Word. That shift of vision from public crowd to holy assembly is the source of the energy to preach. The fire is lit in my belly as I see what the congregation really is, lost people, and what I really have to bring, the life-giving Word.

With everyone saved, though, there was no longer a line to be crossed from death to life. All I could see and all I could preach was what we *should* be doing. We should love one another. We should free one another from dysfunctional entanglements. We should be less prejudiced. We should feed the poor. But all I could say was "We should." I lost the ability to say "You must." Since in the end it didn't really make much difference how people lived, it didn't make much difference what I preached, or if I even preached at all.

My thinking had become frivolous, my theology one of wishful thinking. My words became inconsequential. My religion was reduced to a self-help methodology, a happy way to cope with life. I became a moralist, a counselor, a two-bit pop psychologist.

I took serious steps to leave the ministry. But I felt as if I needed to think through my faith one more time before I junked it all.

Resurrection
When I was a child, my faith hung on the word of older people, parents

and Sunday-school teachers. When I received Christ, my faith hung on my experience of Christ. Following seminary, my faith hung on a theology. Mine was a theology of the Word and the trinitarian nature of God. But that was no longer enough. I could no longer have faith because of my elders, my conversion experience had worn thin, and my theology had led me to universalism, a faith without consequences.

I turned to history for answers. I felt that if I could begin by rethinking my faith not from an experience or a theological concept but from a historical event, just as the Hebrew Scriptures were built on the deliverance from Egypt, then maybe I could rebuild my faith biblically and solidly.

I turned to the New Testament and saw that the first missionaries went out with a message about the crucified and resurrected Lord who was present with them through an outpouring of the Holy Spirit. These missionaries recognized the resurrection as the irreducible, essential element of their faith in Jesus Christ. Their whole lives were built upon the resurrection. Paul puts it squarely: "If Christ has not been raised, your faith is futile; you are still in your sins. Then those also who have fallen asleep in Christ are lost. If only for this life we have hope in Christ, we are to be pitied more than all men" (1 Cor 15:17-19).

I began to ask myself whether I believed in the resurrection of Jesus Christ. It didn't take long to find the answer. It was simple and unequivocal. Though I am a born doubter and have struggled for every inch of my faith, for a reason unknown to me I have never seriously questioned the resurrection of Jesus.

My faith was in about the same shape as the Jerusalem temple—not one stone was left standing on another. But as I surveyed the wreckage, I found that one of the stones of my faith was left in place: the cornerstone, the resurrection of Jesus Christ. From my biblical studies I knew that the resurrection was the cornerstone of New Testament faith; and now I found, unexpectedly, that the resurrection was the irreducible element of my faith as well. So I felt fully justified in rethinking my faith from the foundation of the resurrection of Jesus Christ.

From the perspective of belief in the resurrection, it didn't take me long to realize that I had to take Jesus of Nazareth seriously. After all, the resurrection of Jesus is, among other things, God's specific vindication of Jesus' earthly life and teachings. If God vindicated Jesus in his resurrection, then it was obvious that I needed to take Jesus' teachings seriously, including his eschatology.

This didn't mean that I was ready to accept the existence of hell. I wondered whether the writers of the Gospels had changed Jesus' views on hell. I thought, for instance, that the writer of Matthew, known for his legalism, might highlight hell, while a writer like Luke, known for his urbane inclusiveness and social concern, might lower its profile. I wondered whether Mark, known for terseness, would cut hell out, or whether John, known for a realized eschatology, might remove eternal judgment. So I got out my Gospel synopsis and began to look up the words of Jesus on hell.

I was disappointed, frankly, to see that all the Gospel writers cite Jesus' teachings on eternal judgment. From Gospel to Gospel, Jesus' views on hell remain intact. What I found to be consistently witnessed is that Jesus, the greatest teacher of love in human history, time after time boldly and blatantly used escape from hell as a motivation for moral living.

Jesus' moral teaching had teeth. Dorothy Sayers states it unequivocally:

> There seems to be a kind of conspiracy, especially among middle-aged writers of vaguely liberal tendency, to forget, or to conceal, where the doctrine of Hell comes from. One finds frequent references to the "cruel and abominable mediaeval doctrine of hell," or "the childish and grotesque mediaeval imagery of physical fire and worms." . . .
>
> But the case is quite otherwise; let us face the facts. The doctrine of Hell is not "mediaeval": it is Christ's. It is not a device of "mediae-

val priestcraft" for frightening people into giving money to the church: it is Christ's deliberate judgement on sin. The imagery of the undying worm and the unquenchable fire derives, not from "mediaeval superstition," but originally from the Prophet Isaiah, and it was Christ who emphatically used it. . . . It confronts us in the oldest and least "edited" of the gospels: it is explicit in many of the most familiar parables and implicit in many more: it bulks far larger in the teaching than one realizes, until one reads the Evangelists through instead of picking out the most comfortable texts: one cannot get rid of it without tearing the New Testament to tatters. We cannot repudiate Hell without altogether repudiating Christ.[6]

My own study led me directly to Sayers's conclusion: Jesus believed in hell, and if I wanted to take him seriously in my ministry, I had to take hell seriously. And furthermore, I had committed myself to a ministry of being a parable of Jesus to my people; could I be a parable of Christ if I disregarded one of his major teachings?

But what can hell be? There must be some way to describe it. Here Baron Friedrich von Hügel helped me. I had already read von Hügel on spiritual direction and found his advice critically important. So I looked for his views on hell. He suggests this description of hell:

The lost spirits will persist, according to the degree of their permanent self-willed defection from their supernatural call, in the varyingly all but complete self-centeredness and subjectivity of their self-elected earthly life. But now they will feel, far more than they ever felt on earth, the stuntedness, the self-mutilation, the imprisonment involved in their endless self-occupation and jealous evasion of all reality, not simply their own selves.[7]

A Theology with Teeth

With the resurrection of hell in my theology, my ministry took on new vigor. My preaching became theological again. My preaching got hotter and better. Even the liberals in my congregation liked it better.

What about Calvinism? It had been my belief in predestination that made me initially question the existence of hell in order to relieve the unbearable tension of double-predestination.

My Calvinism has not changed. I haven't got it figured out yet. What has changed is that I no longer need my theology to be all figured out. I don't mind the paradoxes. Theology with paradox is the only kind with room for God.

With hell kicked back into my theology, something unexpected happened. It was to be expected that my evangelistic preaching would get hotter. What I hadn't anticipated was that my preaching and teaching on social issues and concerns got hotter too. After all, Jesus himself taught us to care for the poor and oppressed. Yet his teaching on the subject, like that of the prophets, was based squarely on the fact that *those who refuse to care for the needy will be judged*. He presented the issue unequivocally when he described the fate of those who had refused to care for the needy:

"Lord, when did we see you hungry or thirsty or a stranger or needing clothes or sick or in prison, and did not help you?"

He will reply, "I tell you the truth, whatever you did not do for one of the least of these, you did not do for me."

Then they will go away to eternal punishment, but the righteous to eternal life. (Mt 25:44-46)

What an irony: many social-activist Christians have rejected the doctrine of eternal punishment because they think it detracts from social concern. But if Jesus' words are taught straight from the Gospels, social concern will become central to every Christian, since our eternal destiny hangs in the balance.

I scorched some eyebrows when I preached that racial prejudice and anti-Semitism could send a person to hell. The congregation knew I meant it. And they took it, because I was preaching the Word of God from a prophetic position of declaring God's judgment against sin.

I think the widespread universalism among social-justice Christians declaws their message. Universalism takes all the gravel, bite and guts out of the movement and makes its preaching soft, sentimental and hyperglycemic.

During those precious minutes of the worship service when the congregation isn't looking at me, I don't see "saved" and "unsaved" people. I don't calculate salvation. I can't reduce salvation to any form of sacramental security, whether it is walking forward to take Communion or walking forward to accept Jesus. All I see is people that need Christ. I see people in danger. I feel a fire light in my gut: the message God has given me for this morning is something the congregation needs to hear and respond to. Nervousness about my performance is displaced by concern for the people to hear the Word of God and believe in faith. I see their end. I see their need. I see that there is a decision to be made about Christ, and that decision counts for everything.

With his eschatology firmly in hand, Jesus went forth to preach.

After John was put in prison, Jesus went into Galilee, proclaiming the good news of God. "The time has come," he said. "The kingdom of God is near. Repent and believe the good news!" (Mk 1:14-15)

VI

Preaching

Then the LORD spoke to you out of the fire.
You heard the sound of words but saw no form;
there was only a voice.

DEUTERONOMY 4:12

*T*hree thousand people heard the hellfire preacher. His presumption was our damnation. His sermon drew a line in front of each of us and delivered a summons: *Cross it.* The line separated death and life. We were on the side of death. We needed to cross the line to life.

This was assault and battery on my integrity. I was an acolyte. I resisted the demand with all my will. I did not flinch before the outrage. He said I was going to hell. He demanded that I accept Jesus Christ as my Lord and Savior. He called me forward. Some migrated to the stage. I sat. Sweat precipitated on my brow. I was boiling. I shook. The line was still there. He insisted: *Cross it.*

A corn-syrup voice I did not trust interrupted from beside me: "We will wait for you if you go forward." It was my friend's mother. This was a setup. They'd known there was going to be an altar call, and they expected me to go forward. They didn't think I was a Christian. My refusal redoubled. I stared the line down.

At home, in bed, in the dark, in shock, I thought it through. I was proud of myself for not joining the mob that had surged forward. But the line was still there.

It was no longer drawn on the stage, it was scratched in my soul. The demand remained: *Cross it.* I was afraid. My potent debunking of that gospel-carnival-of-the-absurd was impotent when applied to the gospel message.

I sensed God's presence, but how could this be God? Up till now *God* had always meant that everything I did and thought was secure and good. Now *God* meant that I was lost. My mind clouded and spun in spiritual vertigo. There were no reference points left in my soul—except the line. I refused to cross it. I would not admit that the hellfire preacher was right about anything.

I felt a logical distinction begin to emerge just beneath the surface of my consciousness. I couldn't read it, but I knew that it was there. It suggested reality, so I followed the trail. My will dragged my consciousness into the mental crevasse.

What I saw was that my anger at the gospel sideshow was valid, but my refusal to cross the line and accept Jesus Christ was stubborn pride, maybe even deadly pride. I'd never seen deadly pride in me. It scared me to think that there was something in me that could will my death. I no longer saw the preacher calling me. It was God calling me to cross the line. Still I refused.

Then, accountably, I began to fear my pride more than the humiliation of crossing the line. The superstructure of my will began to collapse. My world was passing away.

The voice summoning me to cross the line softened its tone but increased its urgency. I knew that I was in danger. The call sounded like love. The line became a mercy; a light gathered at the source of the voice on the other side of the line. My mind's eye fixed on the light.

"Jesus, I don't know what I'm doing, but I accept you as my Lord and

Savior, whatever it means."

Calm came, the light gave way to a peaceful dark, I fell asleep.

The next morning I testified to my friend who had conned me into going to the crusade: "That preacher is a phony. He deliberately turned the air conditioning off so that he could manipulate the crowd."

Now I myself am a preacher. I don't use the methods of the hellfire preacher; I deplore all manipulative methods. But my struggle with Christ on that night, initiated by that man's preaching, is gold to me. It is the treasury out of which I coin my own preaching. It represents the turning point in my life, when Christ fought me and saved me.

The line the preacher drew long ago is engraved in my soul; it is spiritual scar tissue. The deep bruise on Jacob's tendon, brought in mortal conflict with the angel, left him limping; my soul's incision, brought in mortal conflict with Christ, left me preaching. The essence of the line in me is a personal knowledge that pervades my preaching: There is a decision to be made about Christ.

This personal knowledge is my interpretive principle, my hermeneutic, when I prepare my sermons and when I preach. It's as if the line is drawn on a kind of computer chip inside me. It's a "hermeneutical chip"—it processes Scripture into a sermon and drives the sermon in preaching. When preaching goes stale, the recovery of the hermeneutic is the key to revitalization.

The pastor's hermeneutic contains the pastor's eschatology as it is understood intellectually *and* as it is known from experience with the gospel. John the Baptist's eschatology was his message: "Who warned you to flee from the coming wrath? Produce fruit in keeping with repentance" (Lk 3:7-8).

Jesus preached the gospel of the kingdom, an eschatology of change: "Blessed are the meek, for they will inherit the earth" (Mt 5:5).

In his Pentecost sermon Peter preached an eschatology of the crucified and risen Lord, Jesus Christ:

"Therefore let all Israel be assured of this: God has made this Jesus, whom you crucified, both Lord and Christ."

When the people heard this, they were cut to the heart and said to Peter and the other apostles, "Brothers, what shall we do?"

Peter replied, "Repent and be baptized, every one of you, in the name of Jesus Christ for the forgiveness of your sins. And you will receive the gift of the Holy Spirit." (Acts 2:36-38)

Preparing the Word

Tuesday, first thing, I open the text. For an hour I want to be alone with the text. I read it over, stop and stare at it.

Stare: "to look fixedly often with wide-open eyes, to fasten an earnest and prolonged gaze on an object."[1]

I put the text on the computer screen. I fiddle with it. With a computer, experimenting with paragraph breaks is easy. Maybe an idea for a sermon presents itself, maybe not. The only rule for Tuesday is "Do not rush."

Greek and Hebrew look like piles of seaweed to me, but I open the text in the original language and try to work through it with the help of the English. I don't think I can make a better English translation. I don't expect to overturn scholarly exegesis with my word studies. Reading the text in its original languages accomplishes two vital things. Looking at the text in its original tongue is another way to fiddle with it. It is a way of spending unhurried, inefficient time with the text. It forces me to slow down and listen more intently. It's a way of chewing on it. This slow work with the text produces the second benefit of original language study: pictures. Ancient Hebrew and Koine Greek are rich in pictures and metaphors. The pictures underlying the words (especially the theological terms) freshen theology and deliver natural images for preaching.

I own many commentaries, and I use them in my sermon preparation, but I wouldn't trade my Greek and Hebrew Bibles for a thousand commentaries.

I leave my desk and take a walk. I let the text as I can see it—divided into paragraphs, filled with pictures—settle into my mind. I let the text sit in my skull right behind my eyes. I want the text in my subconscious. It takes time to get it there. Walk and pray and leave it alone. When the visual picture of the text disappears from my mind's eye, I return to my desk.

Wednesday and Thursday: I stare at the text more. The word *stare* is a Latin word related to the Latin word for "strenuous." Staring at the text is strenuous meditation. This strenuous meditation is done inside us, in our hermeneutical chip. Staring at the text puts it in the chip, and that's where the work gets done.

A theologian describing hermeneutics is like a physiologist describing running: both use big words to describe a common experience. We all know how to run, but we can't describe how we do it. It's the same with hermeneutics. We pastors do hermeneutical work all the time, but we can't describe it. Hermeneutics is as primitive to humanity as running.

Hermeneutic is our ability to understand a story and tell it to someone else in our own words. Hermeneutics happen at the Main Street coffee shop where the good old boys gather to chew tobacco and cuss government. They read the newspaper story about taxes going up, they process it, and they tell it to each other in their own words. They know what the story means: less money for chewing tobacco.

People do pretty well using everyday hermeneutics with the Bible. It's tougher than the newspaper, because its stories happened a long time ago and customs were different. There's no chewing tobacco in the Bible, but there are taxes. Bible farmers didn't have tape decks in their harvesters, but they had to sow, reap and pray for rain just like today. For the most part, normal people understand the Bible pretty well with the same commonsense hermeneutics they use every day.

Preachers need more than just a commonsense hermeneutic when they read the Bible for sermon preparation. They aren't reading the

Bible for themselves or to teach a Bible study. A sermon is not thoughts about the Bible. Preachers make war on the human heart. Preaching hermeneutics prepare a pastor to decry sin, to look into the eyes in the pews and say with Nathan the prophet: "Thou art the man!"

Pastors take the message of the text and pass it through the logic of their hermeneutic. A computer chip is a thin silicon wafer with a specific logic etched into it by a laser beam. When information is put into the chip, the chip's logic rearranges the information into a different form, but one that corresponds logically to the input. A computer chip can take the input "2 + 2" and process an answer: 4. The logic of the computer chip processes the input and, in a sense, tells the story in its own words.

Preachers' hermeneutical chip is the line embedded in their soul, etched by the laser beam of the Word of God on the day they heard the Word and obeyed the summons. This chip processes the Word of God in Scripture and transforms it into the Word of God that will be preached.

Computer chips get hot—they use energy—because processing the input and rearranging it into a new form is a lot of work. Likewise, sermon meditation takes time, and it is hard work. Just sitting there (looking like you're doing nothing), contemplating the Scriptures, is some of the hardest work of the week. Rushing through Scripture meditation causes shallow sermons.

Friday: More than anything, I pray. I pray a simple prayer over and over: "Lord, of all the things I can say about this text, what do your people need to hear this week?"

I add a variable at this point to my meditation on the text. I begin to consider what I've heard from my people all week. I spend much of my pastoral time listening to people, trying to crack the code of their lives. I hear about their progress in Christ and the sin that drags them down.

I want the biblical text to be the primary input to the sermon. However, the input of the congregation is crucial to the process, because I need to know what kinds of decisions they need to make to follow Christ. I need to know where and how the line must be drawn.

The sermon will, if properly prepared and delivered, be able to encourage the people of God in their progress, admonish them to turn from their sin and introduce some to Christ for the first time. I know that it is possible to accomplish all these agendas in every sermon, because the text contains the code that meets the needs of every heart present. This is the presupposition of biblical expository preaching.

The prayer and meditation continue, working with the Scripture, the people's needs and everything in the hermeneutical chip, every aspect of every variable, to create an answer, the sermon, the biblical story in new words—new words that will be the Word of God preached. Meditation is hard work.

Slowly the sermon emerges. I think best in outlines, so I try to develop a coherent outline for the sermon, correlating the elements of the sermon to the order of the text.

In any case, the most important aspect of the sermon is the thesis. The thesis contains the indicative and the imperative of the sermon. The indicative is the sinners' condition and God's provision for sin; the imperative is the demand that one redress sin by crossing the line, coming to Christ for renewal and repentance.

Once I have the thesis and a simple outline, Friday's work is done.

Saturday: I forget about the sermon and do something with my kids.

Sunday: I rise early to read the Bible and pray. I review the outline and touch it up. Sometimes I throw the outline out and construct a new one.

Delivering the Word

We all know what it is to play warfare in a mock battle, that it means to imitate everything just as it is in war. The troops are drawn up, they march into the field, seriousness is evident in every eye, but also the courage and the enthusiasm, the orderlies rush back and forth intrepidly, the commander's voice is heard, the signals, the battle cry, the volley of musketry, the thunder of cannon—everything exactly as in war, lacking only one thing . . . the danger. So also it is with playing Christianity, that is, imitating Christian preaching in such a way that everything, absolutely everything is included in as deceptive a form as possible—only one thing is lacking . . . the danger.[2]

In a Roman Catholic hospital in our town, in the elevator hallway, there stands a life-size statue of Mary. Her face is perfect serenity. Her body is upright but not tense. Under one of her feet writhes a thickly muscled serpent; in its open mouth, fangs drip poison.

That's what preaching is. Preaching is stepping on the snake.

Children leave during the hymn that precedes the sermon. I enter the pulpit, read the Scripture and fiddle with my notes as I gather my wits. Nervousness gives way to adrenaline for battle; it swells my awareness. I lift my eyes, open my mouth: the sermon begins.

I've heard of the art of preaching, and I've heard of the art of war. Preparation for preaching and for war requires human creativity. Both activities are acquired crafts. Hand-to-hand combat is not a recital, and neither is preaching. Preaching is an art, but it is not an art show. It isn't a concert, it isn't a speech. Preaching is a form of aggression. As we preach, Yahweh, the God of war, conducts holy war to conquer territory. The field of conflict is the human heart.

I begin slowly, letting the words come as they will, following my outline section by section. I lay the groundwork for the thesis by commenting on the text and introducing the thesis slowly. I methodically scan the eyes in the congregation, reading every reaction.

As the sermon progresses and the thesis is revealed, the congregation divides up, splinters into individuals. Some are comforted, others are in distress. Some are angry or stubborn. I feel the battle engage. A line must be drawn in front of every listener.

One person looks offended. I've touched a nerve in a person who is normally self-possessed. What can I say to offend their pride even more?

This is where preaching really begins. The offense is what counts. Stepping on a snake is an offense to the snake. Its pride must be mortally wounded.

It's easy to back off from the offense. The flesh will scream, and the devil will bare his venom-dripping teeth. The human heart is the most fiercely guarded piece of ground in the universe. The fortress is built up through years and years of self-justification and rationalization. The soul in sin feels alive, but it is dead. The sermon must shed light on the soul's dire circumstances so it may turn from sin and live. The people must hear the indicative of the sermon—"Thou art the man!"—if they are to hear the imperative of the sermon, "Repent and be baptized, every one of you, in the name of Jesus Christ for the forgiveness of your sins. And you will receive the gift of the Holy Spirit."

I feel the offense of the words as they pierce hearts. I cannot stop until the whole truth is known: they are lost. Damnation must be preached. As Forsyth says, "There are not nearly enough preachers who preach, nor people who take home, the reality of damnation, or the connection of liberty with it."[3]

I am a well-educated, mainline denomination preacher, quite shy by nature. I don't give altar calls. But when the battle for the human heart is pitched, the line scratched in my soul by that hellfire preacher leads me unfailingly where the sermon must go. The sermon needs to go to Christ. The line needs to be drawn. The demand needs to be made. Christ crucified must be placarded before every listener. There is a light, a calling, a demand, a raised voice, a pounded fist, the stamp of a foot. The snake is crushed.

Now the gospel. At the right moment, with the end in sight, the gentle voice. The Savior who would never snuff the smoking flax or break the bruised reed must also speak and make the plea for the soul to cross the line to life. Grace comes unexpectedly. The Way presents itself. The law raged, the gospel gently beckons. The law has condemned, the

Savior pleads for mercy and peace. The corridor opens for the listener, the opportunity presents itself: *receive the Savior; cross the line; enter life.*

Recovering the Word

Monday must be quiet and free of work. With Word, Spirit and soul the preacher preaches from a rock. But the rock is gone by Sunday afternoon. Monday I can't remember a word I said. I feel vague embarrassment. The scar in my soul is sore. I'd best go fishing.

My system needs sabbath. If Tuesday's work with the text is to be joy and anticipation, Monday must be restful.

Preaching wanes even when you take good care of yourself. Theology grows stale. Sermons get predictable. Instead of a joy, preaching becomes a burden. Compliments from parishioners help. Continuing-education opportunities for preaching exist. But what helps most is to hear good preaching and read good theology, because the thing that goes haywire in us is our hermeneutic.

A computer chip is etched silicon. Chips hardly ever wear out. The downside of that is that computer chips get outdated rather quickly. They can't be rewritten, so they get thrown out.

The logical instructions in our hermeneutical chip can wear out. Conductivity goes down, which slows down our meditation process, making it more laborious. The instructions can become rutted. We can end up preaching the same thing over and over. The instructions can become overwritten or infected with bad code (such as when the virus of universalism gets into our hermeneutics). The upside to this is that the medium of our hermeneutical chip is malleable. It can be rewritten very easily. We can renew our hermeneutics, and we must. The way we renew the instructions in our hermeneutical chip is to hear good preaching and read good theology.

A pastor friend, now retired from pastoral ministry, used to read a sermon of Alexander Whyte every Sunday morning before he preached.

He did this throughout his ministry. He figured that he needed to hear good preaching himself before he could preach. This was an excellent practice.

Reading Christian literature is enormous help in restoring our preaching. Different pastors prefer different types of literature. But in all cases the point of reading Christian literature isn't to find sermon illustrations or ideas for sermons; it is to renew our hermeneutic.

It works so well that good hard theological reading makes my sermon preparation go faster. I've noticed this for years: two hours spent reading an author like Barth, Forsyth, Edwards or Bonhoeffer on Wednesday saves me hours of sermon preparation on Friday and will produce a deeper, more searching thesis. Such writers teach me to think Christocentrically. Thinking Christocentrically helps me sort through the side issues and leads me straight to the heart of every biblical text and the subject of all sermons: Jesus Christ.

The more searching my understanding of Christ, the better my sermon preparation. Given my antipathy to time management schemes, it's a little hard to admit, but reading difficult theology is one the best time-savers I know.

Jonathan Edwards, St. John of the Cross, Dietrich Bonhoeffer—the range of literature is wide. I find that the theologians worth reading all write about Christ. They all know how to handle a biblical text. More than that, they all know where the danger is in the text, and they are unafraid to expose it. They have a deep innate sense for where the text drastically contradicts our lives and where we are in serious trouble. From their expositions of the text we feel our danger. They step on the snake in us and present Christ to us. They call us to repentance. They summon us from death to life.

Having heard, we believe—then we can preach. This is what renews our hermeneutic: hearing Christ preached and taught by authors and preachers who are unafraid to tell us the truth. And that is the whole point of preaching: to tell the truth boldly and unashamedly.

Hearing the Word

A Christian heavy-metal band and a hellfire preacher came to town to put on a show. The youth group wanted to go, so we took them, with some reluctance. I went in silent protest; I felt this was beneath me, I had passed this kind of thing up long ago. (Thinking back, I'm surprised I didn't scrape my nose on the door header as I entered the arena: my schnoz was in the stratosphere.)

Three thousand kids were there—including my son, sitting beside me, as old as I was when I heard the hellfire preacher who first drew the line for me.

The show began with blinding lights, belching smoke and blasting music that made the Wizard of Oz seem like St. Francis. Since I love rock music (and these guys were good), I had to admit that I enjoyed the first half of the show.

The hellfire preacher came on. He talked about sex. Real frank, honest talk about sexually transmitted disease. No show, just the truth. Then he preached the gospel. He was hot, and I was drawn into it. I knew that I needed to cross the line.

I was tempted to debunk the show just as I had twenty-five years earlier. I could see the showmanship. I could also see that all my hotsy-totsy theologizing wasn't reaching three thousand kids with the gospel of Jesus Christ. I listened.

I was glad my son was there, and I know that I needed to be there. I didn't lean over to him and say, "We'll wait for you if you go forward." He didn't go forward. I didn't go forward. But I crossed the line that night. I think he did too.

VII

Prayer

Jesus often withdrew to lonely places
and prayed.

LUKE 5:16

I suppose the existence of God is the only real issue of the pastoral ministry. Not *whether* God exists, but *where* God is and *what* God is. Both questions are answered in the friendship of God experienced in prayer. The pastor's life of prayer answers the questions of God's existence on the deepest experiential level. These questions are answered in the pastor's personal life of prayer, and the pastor answers the questions for others through prayer for them.

Which comes first: speech or hearing? In one sense, speech comes first; we say something, and someone hears it. But what makes us want to talk? What makes us think of something to say? Again, the answer seems easy; we have thoughts that we wish to share, so we speak. A thought as simple as *Pass the milk, please* is expressed because we want milk and it is beyond polite reach. On the other hand, would we say "Pass the milk, please" to someone who was stone deaf? Or would we say it to a person surly to the core and unlikely to grant the request? We might just keep the thought to ourselves and go get the milk.

Hearing precedes speech. We speak because someone who wants to listen is present to hear. The vacuum of an ear ready to hear pulls speech out of us. In our best conversations, hearing precedes speech. We seek a friend so that we can talk. We may or may not have a specific subject in mind; we may just want to talk.

When we find a friend and speak to someone glad to listen, our lives open up to us in a new way. Through the loving listening of a friend we gain ourselves. Of course, the greater grace is when we are sought by a friend just because he or she wants to listen to us. That, more than anything, is how we know we are loved. The existence of friendship is revealed to us by listening: the friend will listen.

God's listening creates a vacuum to our soul. We respond with prayer, and in the process we learn that God loves us. God initiates prayer through his listening.

God listens to us at all times, so we can pray at all times. But God's listening is not vague and unspecific. There are times when God specifically wants us to pray. At these times God's listening presence comes to us in a special, gracious act of love.

Our friendship with God, what we call our personal relationship with Jesus Christ, has its experiential reality in those moments when God is present, listening for our prayer. Our lives are drawn out weak and disjointed and given back to us whole.

We need not whip ourselves with guilt because God wants us to pray all the time and we pray so little. Instead, we need to be acutely attentive to the presence of God. If we let go of our assumption that we know when to pray, and let God's presence draw prayer out of us, prayer becomes free and even friendly. The friend does not demand that we speak; the friend creates space so that we may speak. God causes prayer by being the friend who is present, ready to listen, creating space for us to speak.

Prayer and the Existence of God

The corollary to the observation that prayer is caused by God's listening is that we believe in God because we pray. Yes—we believe in God because we pray! This contradicts our normal idea that we pray because we believe in God.

I have said that hearing precedes speech. What precedes hearing? Love. The hearing that draws speech out of us is an act of love from the hearer to us. Love precedes hearing, because all intentional listening that desires to hear is an act of love and therefore an expression of love.

When we speak in response to such hearing, we are responding to hearing as an act of love, and we acknowledge the existence of love. We come to believe in the existence of loving persons because they listen to us in love. We learn this experientially: in their act of listening and through our experience of being listened to, we know that we are loved. The same is true in knowing God.

I have never heard anyone tell me that they decided to believe in God and then decided to pray. Instead, what I hear people telling me is that some kind of extreme circumstance drove them to pray, and that through the act of prayer (even if it did not change the circumstance) they began to know God. Somehow, in the middle of the crisis, they unaccountably became aware that God was there to listen; they prayed, and then they believed.

When our existence is threatened, whether through accident, illness or a sermon, we begin to know for the first time that our efforts to establish our existence are at an end. Only then can we discover that God is there to establish our shattered existence in love, through prayer.

There is an experience of the Spirit of God hovering over the chaos of our lives when we know that God is there to listen.

Deep calls to deep
   in the roar of your waterfalls;
all your waves and breakers
   have swept over me. (Ps 42:7)

We do not feel God's presence as such, we do not hear it, we do not sense it in any normal way. In this event of divine graciousness God comes to us as a profound Absence.

Truly you are a God who hides himself,
O God and Savior of Israel. (Is 45:15)

It is an absence of answers, it is an absence of feelings, it is an absence of knowledge, but it is not an absence we experience as nothingness. We experience it as space for us to speak, and thus it becomes an experience of the love of God.

What is more, love gives us words. The Spirit prays through us, and we know the friendship of God as we are drawn into the love God has within himself. In the friendship of God, God comes to us to listen. We speak, and the Spirit breathes our words to God, and we believe.

"Faith comes from hearing the message," the apostle tells us (Rom 10:17), but *it is equally true that faith comes by being heard*. As the psalmist says, "I love the LORD, for he heard my voice; he heard my cry for mercy" (Ps 116:1).

Through prayer, then, we learn to believe in God, and not just as a theory but as a friend who is present, a friend who listens and loves.

Wandering Prayer

Sometimes my head gets filled with static. My problems are shouting, flaunting themselves above my faith. Self-pity orders my emotions around like a sergeant. My talents scatter before the cacophonous taunts of the enemy: depression.

Years ago I forced myself to work through these times. None of the work I did was worth anything. Eventually I learned that when these feelings come, I must stop trying to work, stop listening to the noise in my head and start paying attention to God. What I inevitably find when I pay attention to God during these times is that he is there, ready to listen. I need to drop everything and pray.

I have a prayer trail. A bare dirt path meanders from my back door through a field of weeds to the crest of a bluff overlooking the Bitterroot River. There the trail disappears. Once I reach the bluff I can head off in any number of directions, and no direction is chosen often enough to wear through the turf. The river bottom is a random dispersion of tall grasses, aspens and cottonwoods, wild rose thickets. I wind my way through them as I think and pray.

There is no destination. Each step is a destination, I take each turn as it comes. Nor is there a specific direction for the prayer. Each word, each thought is its own prayer; the thoughts come as they will. I don't plan the prayer. God's listening draws it out, the Spirit directs it.

Wandering prayer is different from morning prayer. Morning prayer is scheduled and ordered. Wandering prayer isn't scheduled; it is spontaneous. It isn't ordered; the elements are randomly dispersed. Whereas morning prayer is praying the Psalms, wandering prayer is praying *like* the Psalms.

Psalm prayers move effortlessly between talking to God, talking to self and talking to imagined audiences in speech patterns without boundaries.

> The LORD is my shepherd, I shall not be in want.
> He makes me lie down in green pastures,
> he leads me beside quiet waters,
> he restores my soul.
> He guides me in paths of righteousness
> for his name's sake.
> Even though I walk
> through the valley of the shadow of death,
> I will fear no evil,
> for you are with me;
> your rod and your staff,
> they comfort me.
>
> You prepare a table before me

in the presence of my enemies.
You anoint my head with oil;
  my cup overflows.
Surely goodness and love will follow me
  all the days of my life,
and I will dwell in the house of the LORD
  forever.

This montage of metaphors migrates between faith confession, intro-
spective reflection and talk to God. It's all prayer, even though only part
of this "prayer of prayers" is speech addressed directly to God.

Wandering prayer is opening our mind in the presence of God. This
kind of prayer is rambling, wrestling, yielding and revealing. Theologically it is laying one's life before the cross with the awareness that the
Lord of the cross is hearing and interacting. In it church problems are
addressed, sin is confessed, and assurance is given. In wandering prayer
our minds are emptied, understood, reordered and set right. It is our
consciousness and conscience unpacking cargo in the presence of God
for his repacking under the terms of the gospel.

Once in a while, during wandering prayer, another kind of prayer
takes over: silent prayer. No prayer technology can give birth to this kind
of prayer, it just happens. Talking stops; simple, silent awareness of God
begins.

Silent Prayer

I've driven every inch of Interstate 90 from Seattle to Boston, but my
favorite stretch snakes along the Clark Fork River in western Montana
from Superior to St. Regis. The "lower" Clark Fork, as it's called, is about
two hundred yards wide, slow and deep. It has some of the finest dry
fly fishing for wild rainbow trout in the world. Fishermen drive past it,
figuring a river near a freeway can't be any good. That's fine with me.

It was an exceptionally warm March morning, and I was driving to a

meeting in Idaho, so I planned to eat lunch on the river. I pulled off
Interstate 90 near Superior (Sloway exit, for those interested in trying
the fishing) and drove across a field to an abandoned, disassembled
railroad track. This makeshift gravel road sidehills the Clark Fork to an
otherwise inaccessible stretch of the river.

I parked my truck on the two-hundred-foot bluff over the river and
stumbled and slid down the 80-percent-grade gravel hill to the river's
edge. I was not alone. Elk tracks and elk scat were everywhere. An elk
carcass, a winter casualty torn open by ravens, eagles and coyotes, lay
strewn up and down the hillside. Beaver were on the river, slapping the
water to warn their loved ones of my ominous presence.

Sitting on a rock facing the river, I slurped up my yogurt and choked
down my peanut butter sandwich. I prayed as I ate and enjoyed the
welcome spring sun. I still can't believe I hadn't brought my fly rod, but
I did have a copy of John Donne's "Divine Poems." I read:

> Heare us, O Heare us Lord; to thee
> A sinner is more musique, when he prayes,
> than spheares, or Angels praises bee,
> In Panegyrique Alleluias;
> Heare us, for till thou hear us, Lord,
> We know not what to say;
> Thine ear to'our sighes, teares, thoughts gives voice and word.
> O thou who Satan heard'st in Jobs sick day,
> Heare the self now, for thou in us dost pray.[1]

Thinking stopped, talking stopped. The sun embraced me, and a million
tiny mayflies hatched off the river. They shimmered in the rays of light
as the breeze moved them to and fro. God's benign presence warmed
me from within. God told me that he loved me and that I was on the
right track. I did not block the experience with chatter, but silently
relished it. Time became an irrelevant coordinate. Was it thirty seconds?
Thirty minutes? The experience passed on its own terms, just as it came.

Where is God? Right here. What is God? God is love.

I rose from the rock and climbed the steep hill to my car with a deep gladness. I didn't even care anymore that I was going to a committee meeting.

The Grammar of Pastoral Prayer

When I began pastoral ministry, the most formidable element of Sunday worship was the pastoral prayer. In preaching I wield a tool, but in prayer I open my heart. Prayer is an intimate event. I didn't like baring my soul before God in public. My tongue tied. Wandering prayer didn't work. Using psalms and other Scripture helped, but pastoral prayer is more than reading prayers. It took parenthood to teach me how to pray for my people.

The grammar of pastoral prayer can best be described as parental. On that account it is no anachronism that priests are called "Father." For the priestly role is preeminently, more than just by analogy, the parental role. As it is said of Job, "Early in the morning he would sacrifice a burnt offering for each of them, thinking, 'Perhaps my children have sinned and cursed God in their hearts.' This was Job's regular custom" (Job 1:5).

How do you pray for your children? If you don't have children, how do you imagine you would pray for them?

Christian parents pray for every aspect of their children's lives. They pray for their health and for success in their school and careers. If their child is ill, they pray with urgency for healing. If their son or daughter is up for a scholarship or a job promotion, they pray they receive it. Parents don't have to pray fair.

Christian parents pray for their children to follow Christ. They pray that their children's sins be forgiven. They pray for God to have mercy on their children. They pray for their children's character development.

A parent's prayer begins with the indicative, "Lord, my child is sick," and moves swiftly to the imperative, "Lord, heal my child." It stays in the imperative until the parent's heart is emptied. In parental prayer, the imperative is the dominant mood.

Parents must be open to God's will and must teach their children that God's will might be other than their will, but parents don't qualify every request with "Thy will be done." Parents advocate for their children in prayer, and must not be ashamed to do so. They must advocate urgently and vehemently and allow God to deal with their prayers as he will. They remind God of his great acts of salvation and ask him to apply them to their children. Parents use God's promises in their prayers. They remind God of his promises; they hurl God's promises at him in their prayers.

This intercession is deeper than the prayers we pray for ourselves. Parents pray for their children with a love that is simple and unqualified.

The key to the parent's prayer is the love. Love subjects the parent to the child's need to such an extent that the parent enters the Absence facing the child. The prayer is drawn out of the parent in response to the space created by the Absence, which is, of course, the ear of God listening.

Pastoral prayer begins with indicatives. In praise and thanksgiving we declare God's blessings. We confess our sin. We state our circumstances. It moves quickly to the imperative. Like the parent's prayer, the heart of pastoral prayer is the imperative.

A pastor's prayer is unashamed advocacy. When the Lord was angry with Israel, "Moses sought the favor of the LORD his God" on their behalf (Ex 32:11). Moses pleaded and bargained with God to save the people of Israel. It worked. The Lord relented of his plan to destroy the people. Psalm 106 tells us that in his prayers Moses "stood in the breach before him to keep his wrath from destroying them" (Ps 106:23).

Pastoral prayer does not flinch from using direct, unqualified imperatives: "Give us this day our daily bread." Pastoral prayer is persistent, argumentative, importunate. Pastors pray insistently and never give up.

Then Jesus told his disciples a parable to show them that they should always pray and not give up. He said: "In a certain town there was a judge who neither feared God nor cared about men. And there was a widow in that town who kept coming to him with the plea, 'Grant me justice against my adversary.'

"For some time he refused. But finally he said to himself, 'Even though I don't fear God or care about men, yet because this widow keeps bothering me, I will see that she gets justice, so that she won't eventually wear me out with her coming!' " (Lk 18:1-5)

Normally we pray in the first person: "Forgive us our debts as we forgive our debtors." That is necessary and appropriate. But there is also a place for "Forgive them, Father, for they know not what they do."

The tenderest element of pastoral prayer is intercession in the third person. This happens when the grammatical person shifts from the first-person plural to the third-person singular and the third-person plural. Not "Heal us," but "Heal John." Not "Forgive our sins," but "Forgive their sins." Not "Pour out your Holy Spirit upon us," but "Pour out your Holy Spirit upon them." The pastor must become an advocate for the congregation and plead with God wholeheartedly on behalf of the beloved.

A lot of pastors are afraid to pray this way, because they fear it might make them sound arrogant, as if they themselves don't need forgiveness or the outpouring of the Holy Spirit. But if the congregation knows the pastor's humility and love, they will accept intercessory prayer as the most tender and humble element of pastoral prayer.

The turning point in any pastoral prayer is when the pastor enters the Absence created by God's listening before the congregation and prays within that space. The congregation is a chaotic soup of need. The Spirit of God hovers over the waters. When the pastor feels this need and enters into it and prays out of it, love for the congregation is driving the prayer. The pastor's heart is opened. People come to believe in God during prayer like that.

Once I learned how to pray for my people in public, I knew how to pray for them privately. On my wandering-prayer walks I move in and out of prayer for myself, intercession for my family and friends and intercession for my congregation.

Pinpoint Prayer

"Willie Barnett just had surgery for cancer; she's pretty serious," a nurse in the church told me.

"Who is Willie Barnett?" I asked.

"A woman who used to go to our church."

I pondered the information skeptically. Almost everybody in this town "used to go to our church." I didn't know Willie Barnett, and I didn't know if I wanted to know her. I didn't know if she wanted to know me.

I pray with my parishioners—that is a given—but I don't visit every cancer patient I hear about. What about this cancer patient? I'm not called by God to pray for everyone. I wish it were clear to me who God wants me to pray for. Instead, I usually just stumble into these things and hope it's God's will.

I don't remember why I decided to visit Willie. Maybe I figured I'd end up doing her funeral. Maybe I happened to be at the hospital for another visit and so I stopped by. Anyway, there was no sign from heaven that I was supposed to pray for her.

I walked into her room and guessed she was in her late sixties. She was definitely in pain. I didn't know if it was the right time to be there or not, so I looked into her eyes for a sign. They didn't read "Get the hell out of here." So I proceeded to initiate a visit, slowly.

"I'm Pastor Hansen from the Florence-Carlton Church. I hear you've had surgery. What's your situation?"

"Pastor, I've had surgery for a bowel blockage, and I have ovarian cancer. A year ago I had surgery for uterine cancer. As soon as I recover from this surgery, they'll start me on chemotherapy." She winced through her pain and teared up.

I recoiled, thinking: *Chemo. Poison. Rotting guts.* I wasn't planning on staying long.

"May I pray for you?" I inquired.

"Oh yes, please do, Pastor. I need prayer," she pleaded, her voice cracking with emotion.

I prayed for her. It was simple, direct, short. Afterward her eyes glistened, and through the anguish I saw hope.

I visited Willie and her husband three months later in their home. We talked about her situation. She was ashamed of her hair loss, and the chemo was working on her digestive tract, making her nauseated. Her prognosis was not good. It was all wait and see.

She and her husband raised sheep. They were lambing at the time, and she hated not being able to help out. She had grown up on a farm, so she was well acquainted with life's beginnings and endings. She was not afraid to die, but she loved life and wanted to live. We prayed for healing.

I visited many other times. Each time we talked, I read Scripture and prayed. The more I visited, the more I was able to enter into the prayer with my own love for Willie and her husband. I began to allow myself to feel their pain and pray out of my sense of their pain. Those prayers connected.

Six months after they began, the treatments ended, and Willie was declared clean of cancer. She told me many times that there was no question in her mind that the prayers healed her. Not many women survive ovarian cancer, so I wasn't going to argue. They started coming to church faithfully and made many Christian friends.

A few years later, coming through the line after worship, she shook my hand and her eyes were wet.

"I have to go in again," she said gravely. "I have a tumor on my intestine."

When I visited her in the hospital, she cried when she saw me: "I had to have a colostomy." I leaned down and gave her a hug and a kiss. We visited some, and I prayed for her.

It was easy to pray with Willie and her husband. We were good friends by now. Every time we prayed we felt closer to one another and to God. We felt more and more sure that God was at work healing. I visited her and prayed for her all through her chemotherapy and the humiliating months of adjustment with the bags and appliances.

She got well again, giving the glory to God and the power of prayer. She and her husband remained faithful worshipers.

Three years later, as we shook hands after worship, I saw the wet, helpless eyes again and knew something was wrong. She was to have surgery again. More cancer.

When I visited her in the hospital after her surgery, I thought she was going to die. She was too exhausted to cry. We prayed, and again, through the pain, I could see the hope. This woman believed in God.

The recovery and the chemo were especially tough this time. She was having trouble keeping food down; her hair was gone. She was jumpy, itchy, numb and limp. She felt as if her nervous system was corroding. Praying was tougher this time.

This was a summer of drought in Montana, the summer of the great fires in Yellowstone. The streams were drying up, the forests were burning down. It was a summer of drought for our prayers too; our faith was arid. We prayed together, but none of us wanted to enter into the pain. Praying in the space given to us by God left us feeling dead. We had no assurance that God was at work.

I knew that Willie loved right-out-of-the-stream, pan-sized trout, so one day, instead of going to her house and praying for her, I went to the wilderness and fished for her. My goal was five small Western Slope Cutthroat trout. The year previous I had caught and released seventy trout in three hours at Boulder Creek, so that's where I headed.

Boulder Creek was reduced to a trickle of tepid water. I came away with three fish. Three creeks and four hours later I had my five fish.

When I arrived at Willie's, I didn't stop in and pray with her; I just handed her a plastic bag filled with five slimy fish. She wept for joy as she clutched the bag. That evening she fried them in cornmeal and a little butter and ate them up. Many times later she claimed that those fish were the turning point in her recovery.

Today Willie is healthy; she knows that God has healed her. Her doctors told her as much: "Someone up there is looking after you." I'm not so certain. I don't jump to conclusions about prayer. But I'm glad I prayed for her. When I look at it rationally, I realize that if I hadn't prayed for her, she probably would have died.

VIII

Friendship

I no longer call you servants. . . .
Instead, I have called you friends.

JOHN 15:15

*J*esus called sinners friends. His enemies accused him of being a friend to sinners: "Here is a glutton and a drunkard, a friend of tax collectors and 'sinners' " (Lk 7:34).

The New Testament corroborates that Jesus was a friend to sinners. He visited with them on the streets, called them as disciples, attended their parties and invited himself over to their houses for dinner. In friendship Jesus shared the gospel. Jesus' friendship with sinners was an "enacted parable expressing his message that God makes himself the Friend of sinners."[1]

Jesus made house calls. Jesus' friendship meant, specifically, following his friends to their home.

Jesus sought Levi in his place of work, while he was collecting taxes, and said, "Follow me." Levi left his booth and followed Jesus. *Then Jesus followed Levi.* Levi invited Jesus to a big dinner at his home. At the party

Jesus fraternized with Levi's friends, and they became Jesus' friends too.

Jesus greeted Zacchaeus in the tree and invited himself over to Zacchaeus's house for dinner. The effect upon Zacchaeus was profound. His friendship with Jesus prompted repentance:

> Zacchaeus stood up and said to the Lord, "Look, Lord! Here and now I give half of my possessions to the poor, and if I have cheated anybody out of anything, I will pay back four times the amount."
>
> Jesus said to him, "Today salvation has come to this house, because this man, too, is a son of Abraham." (Lk 19:8-9)

Jesus sought and saved the lost through his friendship. He entered homes to heal the sick and to teach. He made wine at a wedding of a friend. He helped some unlucky fishermen keep from getting skunked. He received a costly act of love from a woman at the house of a Pharisee.

His friendship brought him to the cross. The cross was itself the climactic act of his friendship for sinners. On the eve of his crucifixion Jesus told his friends: "Greater love has no one than this, that he lay down his life for his friends" (Jn 15:13).

Jesus' style of entering homes and eating with sinners was carried on by his disciples after his death. In Acts the disciples entered the homes of pagans, to share meals and the gospel. Those whom the disciples befriended followed Jesus.

When Jesus befriended sinners, they followed him. When the disciples befriended sinners, they followed Jesus. When the "enacted parable" of Jesus' life of friendship was taken over by his disciples, they became enacted parables of Jesus. Jesus fully intended his disciples to spend the rest of their lives befriending sinners.

Nancy

I agreed to the wedding on a day I was too weak to say no. I didn't know the family. The mother of the bride called me, prefacing her request with remarks about how long the family had lived in our town, how many people in the church they knew and how highly I'd been recommended. She appealed to my sentimentality. Her daughter and the fiancé lived in California, and her daughter wanted to be married in her hometown. The mother twanged a fear-string in me: as I listened to her I wondered if church members might be disappointed if I refused to do the wedding. So I said yes.

It was a Christmas wedding. It's fun getting to know the people at weddings. The bride's father was Danish, a large-boned, gray-bearded man who rode a big motorcycle. Her mother was attractive, quiet and in control. Her eldest sister Nancy was a sight. The moment I saw her I knew she had cancer. Her gaunt face was liquid and drawn down; her skin was yellow-greenish gray. Under her ears, down her neck to her shoulders, lymph nodes protruded from her skin like saddlebags. We spoke briefly.

You could have shot me with a gun when Nancy showed up in church a couple of Sundays later. Her five-year-old boy was with her. I greeted her as she went through the line, expecting never to see her again. But she kept coming. After six weeks of attendance I asked if we could meet for lunch. She agreed and seemed pleased to be asked.

At lunch we talked about her son, Jacob. She had never married and was about fifty, but had wanted a child; so she had adopted him. She brought up an interest in prayer and the Bible. She admitted she knew little about God. She asked if I could teach her to pray, so we decided to get together once in while to talk about prayer. She also wanted to know about healing prayer.

"Why do you want to know about healing prayer?" I asked her.

She had not yet brought up her illness.

"Because I'm sick . . . I have cancer!" she responded angrily.

She governed herself quickly and told me her story: Leukemia had taken control of her lymph system. She was still taking chemotherapy, but it wasn't working.

"I'm not ready to go. I just don't believe it's time for me to die," she said.

I gave her some ideas about how to begin to pray and study the Bible, and told her that I would pray for her healing.

She kept coming to church. She joined the adult Sunday-school class and enjoyed it very much. We got together once a month or so. We talked about her son, the Bible, prayer. She wanted to know how to become a Christian.

Nancy was a manager. Before her illness she had held management positions in state government and had won numerous awards for her efficient, creative work. Her life was organizing people and programs. Now she faced something she could not control. The doctors took her off the chemotherapy. She could no longer manage her life, because her cancer was unmanageable. So she became a disciple.

Her health deteriorated. She carried oxygen with her. She didn't give up hope for healing. We continued to pray for God's healing touch.

The Montana sky was big and July-blue, and the water was clear and cold for our annual river baptism. Fish were rising. Twelve people were baptized that day. Last came Nancy. Barefoot, in a long skirt, separated from her oxygen, she stepped carefully into the water, barely keeping her balance. She drew to my side, calf-deep in the water.

"Nancy, do you confess Jesus Christ to be your only Lord and Savior from sin?"

"I do."

My vocal chords froze up. With a strained, cracked voice I said: "Then I baptize you, my sister, in the name of the Father and of the Son and of the Holy Spirit."

Reaching down into the stream that gives our arid valley life, I lifted some water in my cupped hands and poured it over her head.

She burst into laughter as the water splashed over her face and down her neck. We all laughed through moistened eyes; then spontaneously we settled into a deep quiet. Something important had just happened. We got out of the way while God touched her.

In September I visited her in the hospital. Her eyes were weary and afraid; she forced a smile. Her abdomen was swelling.

"Yesterday I was at Safeway in the checkout line," she said, "and all of a sudden I stiffened uncontrollably. It was a seizure. I was helpless. Fortunately the checkout lady called an ambulance right away. I was so embarrassed."

She was scared, embarrassed and mad. She could no longer drive—a substantial loss of self-determination. We talked about how sad it was to lose the ability to drive.

Suddenly she began to stiffen. Her jaw set, her teeth clenched, and she shook violently. I called the nurse. She was seizing up. I held her firmly as the nurse administered a relaxant. When it took hold, Nancy passed out. I left stunned and hurt, praying.

A few days later, a friend of hers and I witnessed her signature on her living will.

After that she stayed at her parents' house. Her midsection was bloated. The abdominal lymph nodes had gone berserk; they were the size of footballs. She was tired. We talked about incidental things, but I knew the conversation could not last long, so I addressed the business at hand.

"Nancy, your time has come, hasn't it? You're going to die soon."

"Yes, I know."

"Nancy, now you need to look to Christ all the time. He is a gentle and loving Savior, and he is with you now, more than at any time in your life."

"Yes."

"Nancy, I will be your friend all the way to the end."

"Thank you, I need that very badly."

I prayed and left. Within a week she was dead.

Redefining Our Work

Many pastoral responsibilities fall under the rubric *friend.* Hospital calls, home visits and time spent with parishioners are all acts of friendship.

Hospital visitation is an act of friendship. When you are in the hospital, do you want to see a friend or a religious professional? Good chaplains know how to become a friend. Nobody needs religious professionals. Normal people don't even like them. But everyone wants a friend—a friend is a gift from God. A friend is a parable of Jesus.

Home visitation is an act of friendship. Do you enjoy the serendipitous arrival of a friend? We will drop anything to visit with a friend. A friend's visit is a parable of undeserved grace, an act of love, an unnecessary and lavish show of affection. Whether the mission of the visit is to bring encouragement, to admonish, or to share joy or tragedy, it is the visit of a friend and is therefore enacted grace.

On the other hand, do you enjoy having a quiet evening with your family interrupted by a salesperson at the door? Pastoral calling whose motivation is church growth—visiting to "sell" the church—isn't friendship. It's peddling.

Instead of working for a living, I get paid to go fishing. Most men in our church love to fish. It's tough floating down a crystalline river past deer, mink and herons, casting to three-pound wild trout. But as an evangelist I get more mileage sitting in a river boat talking to a man about Christ than I do by sitting in his front room with his wife hanging over us hoping I can make her husband come to church. I don't consider that to be an evangelistic atmosphere.

A sweaty locker room after a basketball game is an evangelistic atmosphere. Laughing with golfers who are trying not to cuss in the presence of "a man of the cloth" is an evangelistic atmosphere.

When I arrived at the parish, not a lot of men my age attended church. Many fishing trips later, the church is full of men learning about Christ.

What does this mean to the definition of our work? Can pastors call friendship "work"?

I doubt that we can. I don't think of friendship as work. I tell people that I read the Bible, pray and visit with friends. That's all I do. It's not work. It's tiring at times. But we shouldn't expect people to call what we do work. It's better to recognize that our friendship is essentially unnecessary to people. As Kierkegaard said, "A friend is not what we philosophers call the necessary other, but the superfluous other."[2]

Just as wildflowers are superfluous splashes of color strewn by God liberally over a mountain, our friendship is based on the reality of God's unfettered, outrageous desire to bless. It is utterly free, not based on any necessity of created reality. Salvation exists by the free grace and love of God. God's grace works its way out in pastoral friendships; spontaneous, liberal, unnecessary.

Jake

Jake walked into our little country church looking like one of the young men who might have built it a hundred years ago. He was dressed in blue jeans, cowboy boots, a white shirt and a black coat and tie; his angular face suggested a young Johnny Cash. He was tall, slender and straight as a rail. We visited before service. He was a hard-rock miner from Leadville, Colorado. He came a few Sundays and then stopped.

A year later I saw him in Missoula, in a crowd. I sought him out, said hello, but he greeted me with a slightly suspicious eye. Another year went by.

Then in comes Jake to church one Sunday. This time he kept coming. We visited a little more and discovered we shared a love for bluegrass music, so we decided to get together to pick and grin.

It was delightful. Our voices and guitars matched up well. There's something magical about getting two old Martin D18 guitars together for bluegrass. They harmonize like two old coots swapping stories. They almost play themselves. The music was effortless. We started getting together regularly just for the fun of the music. It was a genuine friendship.

The evangelism was far from effortless. Jake was coming to church and listening carefully. He was never offended when I brought up spiritual things in our conversations, but he was keeping Christ at arm's length. He was well schooled in the good-old-boy method of keeping things on a light level: he agreed with everything I said. He didn't want the conversation to get personal through a question or a disagreement. He wanted Christ, but only in bits. He had lived a pretty crazy life. He didn't know if God could accept him. So we met week after week, spent many hours together, playing music and sharing Christ.

Jake became a Christian. He was baptized, joined the choir and through some exceedingly difficult circumstances has proved that he is a follower of Jesus Christ. Jake and I sang "What a Friend We Have in Jesus" at Nancy's funeral.

Friendship is perhaps the most powerful force in the pastoral ministry. It is also the one most fraught with danger.

People Who Love Pastors (and Also Hate Them)

I'm gun-shy of people who like me too much. I like compliments, but when someone starts treating me like I'm the best thing since indoor plumbing, I step back.

They get this look in their eyes when they say thank you. It isn't adult gratitude or childlike delight. It isn't a fair exchange of human love. They're thanking me, but their eyes are focused past me. They're thanking someone or something else. Maybe an ideal I've resurrected. It's unreal.

The relationship can appear normal. Then, without warning, it shifts. Their talk gets contradictory. They thank Jesus but give me the credit. Their speech is thick with spiritual lingo, but they treat me like I'm their savior. I don't think they're talking about me *or* Jesus. They're talking to someone or something I symbolize to them. Psychologists call this transference.

Psychotherapists recognize that their relationships with patients run on a "double track."

All feelings in relationships as we now understand them run on a double track. We react and relate to another person not only on the basis of our conscious experience of the person in reality, but also on the basis of our unconscious experience of him in reference to experiences with significant people in infancy and childhood—especially parents and other family members. We tend to displace feelings and attitudes from these past figures onto people in the present, especially if the person in the present has features similar to the person in the past.[3]

Pastors, like therapists, evoke feelings in people that go way back into people's past.

Feelings toward the therapist therefore stem not only from the real, factual aspects of the therapist-patient interaction, but also from feelings displaced onto the therapist from unconscious representations of people important to the patient early in his childhood experiences. These displaced or transferred feelings tend to distort the therapist, making him appear to be an important figure in the patient's past; they create in one sense an illusion.[4]

Pastors are special candidates for transference, since they are authority figures.

Although transference reactions occur in all relationships, they occur most frequently and most intensely in relationships with authority.[5]

It is of no little consequence that in some traditions pastors are called "Father." We are authority figures with love, so like it or not, we symbolize parents to people. For adults who have had positive relationships with their parents, this creates little problem. They have respect and love for their parents. Likewise, they have a natural respect and love for pastors.

But in cases where the relationship with the parent was deeply faulted, people develop something like an ideal parental construct and transfer this to anyone like a parent—and especially someone who gives them love as their parent should have in the first place. Parishioners can superimpose this ideal parental figure over the pastor; they "fall in love"—not with the pastor, but with the pastor as the incarnation of their ideal parental figure. Then they shift the monumentally important childhood desire to please their parent, which was never satisfied by their natural parents, onto the pastor.

The compliments come fast and thick, and they express a strong and unreasonable desire to "help out any way they can." They try to work harder than anyone else—and make sure the pastor knows it—to earn the pastor's love. They want the pastor to appreciate them more than all others.

Parishioners caught in this unconscious process may undergo "conversion" experiences. They may experience dramatic changes and testify that they have been touched by God (never forgetting to add that it was through the pastor's ministry). In psychotherapy this is called a "transference cure."[6] They do experience dramatic change, but it is motivated by the desire to please the pastor. The results of these "conversions" diminish with time, especially once the period of intense positive feelings toward the pastor wanes.

And those feelings do disappear. Alongside the deep reservoir of childhood desire to please parents there exists a deep reservoir of anger at parents for all the hurt they caused. This anger has no fixed object. It is anger at parents, but children are not psychologically able to be angry at their parents for very long. Children cannot divorce themselves from the parental love they desperately need by showing or even admitting that they are angry. But they can cut loose on someone who *represents* their parent.

Things can go along fine for quite a while, even years. These people are accustomed to forgiving parental figures, so pastors can fail them now and then and they will forgive. In fact, they will vehemently defend their pastor to others, even when the pastor is dead wrong.

Until something snaps. There is no way to predict what will set it off, but suddenly, without warning, the pastor violates some code. The pastor must pay. These people's anger at their parent is unleashed on the pastor.

The pastor still symbolizes the parent, but now the parent being symbolized has shifted. The pastor is no longer the ideal parental figure the parishioner loves. The pastor is now the failed parent the parishioner hates. Without warning, the pastor who yesterday represented all that was right in the world today represents all that is wrong in the world. From Jesus to the devil in one hour.

Countertransference

Now the pastor experiences the power of countertransference. In psychotherapy, countertransference happens when the therapist transfers feelings from his or her own childhood onto the patient.[7] If the patient is eager to please the therapist, the therapist becomes equally eager to please the patient. This happens to pastors all the time.

Most pastors have a built-in desire to please. A relationship that may be euphemistically called a "mutual admiration society" may well be a pastor and a parishioner who symbolize parents to one another and so work at pleasing each other.

As long as they're together, everything is right with the world. The two can discuss other people (who symbolize siblings they compete with), confident that nothing can get in the way of their admiration for one another. Until the relationship breaks.

When it snaps, it is likely to be the parishioner who attacks the pastor. The parishioner is not more at fault. It's just that the parishioner is not as directly an authority figure to the pastor as the pastor is to the parishioner. Pastors don't need to attack parishioners as authority figures. (That's what denominational officials are for.)

When "transference hell" breaks loose, the pastor caught in countertransference will feel as if his or her guts are being ripped out. Something is dying. What must die in every pastor is the subconscious desire to please people. What must not die is the will to love. There's the risk. ✶

"Transference hell" forces pastors to face the most basic choice they will ever make in the ministry. There are only three options:

(Love not please)

1. Leave the ministry;
2. Stay in the ministry but stop loving people (and become a religious hack); or
3. Grow up.

The last option is the toughest. But growing up brings a remarkable reward for pastors: they become a *parson,* a whole person.

The same set of choices exists for the parishioner. The parishioner must decide whether to leave the church, become an unloving member of the community (often these people remain bitter enemies of pastors their whole lives) or grow up and become a whole person. These crises are fraught with danger and with possibility.

The process of growing up is difficult. It involves not taking these attacks personally. It involves separating ourselves from the need to be liked and admired. It involves allowing people to dislike us intensely and still recognize them as children of God, made in his image. Growing up is making the moral decision to love those who make us their enemy and choosing not to see them as an enemy in return. There is no easy way to come to this place, but every pastor has many opportunities to learn how.

Transference and Sexuality

Like all people, pastors are subject to sexual temptation. Sex is a powerful force in most adult lives. For any Christian committed to biblical sexual standards, it takes prayer, effort of will and intelligent choices to maintain those standards throughout one's life. But pastors have an extra strike against them in this battle.

From time to time they must deal with a strange transference reaction: the creation of forceful erotic feelings in the parishioner toward the pastor.[8] Obviously this situation is heightened when the pastor responds in kind with erotic feelings toward the parishioner, feelings grounded in countertransference. The subterranean powers of transference and countertransference magnify the potential for disaster.

It happens more than anyone is willing to admit. Amazingly, most often it is lived through silently, with grace and dignity by both parties.

The erotic dynamic begins with transference's radical desire to please, but the consummation is grounded in transference's desire to destroy. The lust of transference and countertransference in the ministry is not based on any kind of love whatsoever, certainly not eros. The basis is self-destruction. It's a kind of spiritual suicide. I believe many ministers who have affairs do so in order to get out of the ministry. That they later decide to stay in the ministry and cover the incident up, or repent and reenter the ministry, points to how seriously they miscalculated their deed.

There are intelligent steps the pastor can take to avoid the snare.

Don't try to be a therapist. When pastors try to be therapists, the danger intensifies. One-on-one counseling with members of the opposite sex is a hazardous undertaking for any pastor.

The counseling situation heightens the pastor's already precarious role as a kind, loving authority figure, by adding to it the role of loving confidant. Knowing people's secrets creates a bond that can become a bomb.

Every pastor hears secrets and keeps secrets, but it is simply not true that pastors should hear everyone's secrets. I am very careful about the secrets I listen to. Sometimes I decline to hear them when they are offered.

It is of no little consequence that the biblical word for intercourse is also the word "to know." There is a desire to hear and to know people's secrets which is exciting, even lustful. This is a kind of voyeurism, a sort of intellectual intercourse.

Perhaps the best solution to the erotic feelings created by transference and countertransference is to take steps to avoid transference reactions in the first place.

In some schools of psychotherapy, transference is deliberately engendered and dealt with in therapy. But pastors should never, under any circumstances, attempt to create or enhance transference reactions in parishioners. They do happen, and they can have happy endings, but they should be avoided. The happy endings are rare. How can they be avoided?

Parable or Symbol?

A good pastor is a loving authority figure. That much cannot change. But can a pastor be a loving authority figure and not a parental symbol?

A pastor is not a symbol of God. A pastor is a parable of Jesus Christ.

A symbol stands for something else. It makes an absent thing present to the mind. Words are symbols. The word *carrot* is a symbol. Say the word *carrot* and a picture of a carrot comes to mind.

Symbols have a durable quality: even after they are modified temporarily in a particular context, they tend to revert back to their original meaning. That is, we may read that in a particular circumstance a carrot was discovered that was truly green, but that will not change the word's meaning for us in the future. The word *carrot* will continue to symbolize an orange vegetable.

Physical objects can be symbols. The cross symbolizes Christ's suffering and resurrection. People can be symbols. A judge symbolizes the authority of the law of the state.

A parable, on the other hand, is a comparison in which something well known is compared with something less known for the purpose of permanently altering our understanding of the less-known thing. Jesus said to his listeners, "I am the good shepherd." He used a well-known thing, a shepherd, to illuminate a less-known thing, himself. In addition to illuminating the less-known thing, a parable makes that thing present to the mind of the recipient, but in its changed form.

A symbol brings to mind an object we know, while a parable radically alters what we know about an object. This differentiation is terribly important to the pastoral ministry: symbolizing God is perhaps the greatest source of frustration in the pastoral ministry.

Being a symbol of God is an exceedingly weak pastoral role. Symbols do not change people's minds. Symbols reinforce what people already believe. Pastors who allow themselves to become symbols can't teach people new things about God. Instead, these pastors only symbolize back to people what they already believe about God. Likewise, pastors as symbols of parents are susceptible to the transference of every experience parishioners have ever had with their parents. In symbolism, the power to invest meaning lies in the hands of the recipient. Pastors who are symbols are held captive to the thoughts and prejudices of the people to whom they symbolize God and parent.

People want symbols of God. People want their ideas of God reflected back to them. People want their ideal parental figure symbolized for them. People revere symbols; people will pay for symbols, die for symbols, kill for symbols. The greatest, most continuous pressure in the ministry is to symbolize back to people what they already believe about God. In other words, the greatest constant pressure in the ministry is to become an idol.

Being a parable of Jesus Christ is an exceedingly powerful pastoral role. Parables change people's minds. As a parable of Jesus, the pastor has power, because the pastor is the well-known figure juxtaposed to the less-known figure: Jesus Christ. Through their life, pastors can radically alter the understanding of who Jesus is. A parable doesn't mirror back what is already believed, but challenges current belief, expanding and exploding what was thought to be true. Pastors who are parables of Jesus Christ change people's minds about Christ and bring the real Christ to people.

How can a pastor be a parable of Christ and not a symbol of God? There is a critical difference between symbols and parables: symbols are durable, parables are impermanent.

I will not denigrate the use of symbols. We use religious symbols all the time. The creeds of Christendom were originally called symbols. When we recite them, they bring our faith to us in powerful ways.

Admitting that the sacraments are *more* than symbols, can anyone deny that the Lord's Supper and baptism are symbols of the Christian faith? Our best symbols are the oldest ones. The less we mess with them the better.

The durable quality of symbols has an important religious function. It's wrong for pastors to change creeds, traditions and ceremonies to make them "relevant." We must teach what symbols mean but not change them. We must not change the words of institution at the Lord's Supper. It would be heretical to change baptism's trinitarian formula.

Parables are different. In parables the well-known item of comparison comes and goes; it can be fiddled with and fine-tuned, paraphrased and amplified. Any pastor who changes Jesus' trinitarian baptismal formula should be disciplined, maybe defrocked. And yet it is imperative to retell the parables of Jesus with modern words and examples and to create new parables. In a parable the figure of comparison appears and drops away once the illumination of the less-known figure is gained. The item of comparison is unnecessary, even superfluous, once it has illuminated and delivered the less-known item. In fact, once the well-known item has done its work, it needs to get out of the way, fast.

Pastors, as parables of Jesus, bring Christ to people and then as quickly as possible become unimportant, unnecessary, superfluous to the important thing: the parishioners' relationship with Jesus.

Jesus did something similar himself. Jesus brought God to people and then just walked away. In the Gospels Jesus appears to have virtually no follow-up program! Even with his disciples we see him making a point with them and walking away, leaving them shaking their heads time and again. The key is getting out of the way.

Symbols stand for something; they sit still. The flag hangs from its pole where it can be admired and dwelt upon. Parables wander all over the place, never sitting still long enough for a fixation, frustrating the desire of the recipient to fixate on them.

Pastors can allow themselves to become symbols by allowing people to fixate on them. It is tempting to extend our effect on people long enough to get adulation and to create the appearance that we are necessary to people. We can wave like a flag, but we always end up hanging ourselves. Rather, pastors need to allow their personal effect on people to be powerful, but light-handed and brief. This is what it means for a pastor to be humble. Humble pastors don't hang around for adulation, for then they might become an idol. Becoming an idol is the greatest fear of the humble pastor.

Symbols stick around because they mediate spiritual reality. That's good if the symbol is baptism, which really does mediate a spiritual reality. Parables disappear because they introduce the Mediator. Pastors who believe that Jesus is the Mediator, the true and perfect revelation of God, the second person of the Trinity, are not symbols of God; they are parables of Jesus Christ, who is himself the Mediator, the true way to God.

A pastor cannot be a symbol of God, because God is omniscient, omnipresent and omnipotent. No pastor can be like these unique characteristics of God in any way. A pastor can be a parable of Jesus Christ, the Mediator of God, because Jesus lived the Way of the Cross, a road he commanded us to take—and a road which, when we are filled with the Holy Spirit of God's love, we can take. In so doing Jesus allowed himself to be irrelevant to the world, unnecessary to the world, superfluous to the world. In so doing Jesus made himself more than necessary[9] to the world. He became its Savior. When we allow ourselves to become "fools for Christ" (1 Cor 4:10) on the Way of the Cross, we become parables of Jesus and bring Jesus to people just as his disciples did.

We are not the parable of God; Jesus is the parable of God. People meet the Lord Jesus through us. Knowing Jesus as Lord, they know God.

Pastoral friendships are acts of love, enacted parables of the outrageous love of God. They are unnecessary, serendipitous, grace-filled, undeserved and unexpected. They don't sit still. But their effect extends into eternity.

IX

Sacrament

This is my body, which is for you;
do this in remembrance of me.

1 CORINTHIANS 11:24

Y ou may question why a Baptist like myself calls church ceremonies sacraments instead of ordinances. Since I was confirmed an Episcopalian, was a member of a Presbyterian church and am now a Baptist minister, I figure I have the right to use either term. Besides that, in Montana an "ordnance" is something you shoot from a gun.

The less said explaining the sacraments, the better. Pastors administer the sacraments, and people want to know what they mean, so we do need to explain them. But for the most part I just let the sacraments be. They have their own power. They are older than we are, more important than we are, more powerful than we are, and they will be in the church, serving the church and God's people, long after we are gone. Our job is to administer them as humble servants, prudently, with all the respect, order and modesty they deserve.

The sacraments are elemental. They are elemental to our faith, and they are elemental to the great transitions in our lives. Wisdom, God's great companion in creation, must have formed the earth with the sacraments in mind, and the sacraments with the earth in mind. Our lives are entwined with the sacraments as our lives are entwined with the basic elements of the earth and the life of the earth: water, rock, dust, bread and blood.

Water

Silver-haired Paul didn't own gym trunks, or a swimming suit, or a short-sleeved shirt, or sneakers. Paul was a cowboy, and all he ever wore was blue jeans with a big silver belt buckle, long-sleeved Western shirts and cowboy boots. He took his hat off only for dinner and for church. And for his baptism. Down he came into the river, belt buckle in place, wearing his boots.

As he walked out into the river, his smile was so big an army could've gotten lost in it. His eyes sparkled with the joy of the Holy Spirit. He wanted this more than anything. He was ready to take the ride of his life.

As a young man he'd rodeoed. He was a bull rider. I don't know if you've ever seen bull riding up close. Imagine a thousand-pound garage-door spring exploding between your legs.

Paul rode bull in rodeos all over the country, for crowds hoping to see a man survive the toughest eight seconds in sports. Bulls can't be called for unsportsmanlike conduct. They are the power of death and chaos in animal form. They are cut loose with the fury of a hurricane to see if a man may be the victor over death. In bull riding, man rides chaos in order to defeat it.

Few men will strap their hand to the back of a Brahma bull. In the narrow chute, right before the gate opens and the bull bolts into the arena, the other riders help the competitor get settled onto the animal, wrapping the rope over his gloved hand, tying him down for the sacrifice. In the seconds before the performance the bull writhes, crushing the rider's knees against the fence board.

Paul had won a lot, and he went to Madison Square Garden. His ride at the Garden was short. This time the bull won. Paul wasn't thrown clear. He landed in the churned-up dirt beside the bull. The animal turned on him, rose above him and came down with both front hooves on his breastbone. After crushing his chest, the bull broke his arms. It barely missed his head on a third swipe. The clown drew the bull away so the medics could get in. They thought Paul was dead. He was rushed to the hospital, where only by a miracle he survived.

We can't save ourselves. We can't ride chaos and death and win. We can't go in the grave and come out. We need to follow the path of One able to die and then live. When we publicly take our stand with that One, when we climb into his grave and rise out with his Spirit, we trust our life and our death to his life and his death. Then we no longer need fear death, for through him we have won.

Thirty years after his ride at Madison Square Garden:

"Paul do you confess Jesus Christ to be your only Lord and Savior from sin?"

"I do."

I dunked Paul, all the way under, into the grave of Jesus.

"In the name of the Father and of the Son and of the Holy Spirit."

I pulled him out of the grave, into the resurrection of Jesus.

Sacraments are funny things. They are short and simple, they involve the simplest elements in our environment, they require few words. The more we get out of the way the better. Yet they change people. People remember them for their whole lives.

My eight-year-old daughter was baptized that day along with Paul. Several years later we were driving home from another river baptism, and I asked Laura if she remembered her baptism. Without hesitation she confidently replied: "Oh yes, Daddy, I remember. Because I was baptized, if I die, I don't have to be afraid."

Rock

They wanted to have their baby baptized, so I agreed to visit them. As

I pulled up to their little cabin, I prayed for wisdom. I was new in town and new in ministry. I didn't know the young couple; all I knew is that they didn't attend worship anywhere. I sensed a possibility to share Christ—that's why I went.

They were young, bright and full of hope. He was from the East Coast, she from the Midwest. She was about twenty-two, he about twenty-five. They had both grown up in churches with traditions of infant baptism. Serving two community churches, I had baptized infants of believing parents in my congregations, though I always took the opportunity to talk to them about infant dedication. So that's how I began with this couple.

At the end of my comparison of baptism and dedication, I mentioned that in either case I only baptize or dedicate infants of parents who attend church. In the final analysis their essence is the same: in both baptism and dedication we acknowledge the child as a gift from God and a member of God's household, and we commit ourselves to raising the child in the ways of Christ in his church. Parents who don't attend church can't keep the vow—it's as simple as that.

They began to shift uneasily in their chairs. A barrier had arisen. The young man interrupted me politely and said, "I think you should know that we're not married. We live together."

I changed my tack.

"OK, first we need to get you married and then we can talk about having a baptism or a dedication. No marriage, no baptism."

They became argumentative. He spoke for them: "Just because we're living a certain way doesn't mean that the child should suffer for it. Just because we're living together you shouldn't refuse to baptize our baby."

I replied, "Your child does suffer for what you do and how you live. Baptism or dedication isn't magic. It doesn't make the child into something that it's not. It is recognizing something that the child is, and points the parents in the way they need to be faithful to that child. While you are living together, you cannot raise the child in the ways of Christ.

Living together is a sin. You can't raise the child in Christ while you're living together. No marriage, no baptism."

The conversation became quite strained at this point. I wasn't trying to force them into getting married; I just wasn't going to dedicate or baptize their baby while they were living together. I felt they might be confused about why I was willing to marry them in their present circumstances but not baptize their baby. So I explained the fundamental difference between the two.

"You see, in the Bible, marriage is a creation thing, and baptism is a Christian thing. Marriage is instituted at the beginning of creation; it applies to all people everywhere, regardless of their religious affiliation. Baptists and Buddhists and atheists and Muslims all need to get married instead of living together. It's built into the way God made humankind. I do marriages for people who are not Christians because I'm helping people do the right thing according to the Bible. God instituted marriage, and I am a person who carries out God's institutions, so I marry people.

"Baptism, on the other hand, is specifically a Christian thing. It isn't for everyone. Only Christians should be baptized, and only children of Christians should be baptized or dedicated. In baptism we publicly confess Christ as Savior and Lord; this means that we trust Christ for our salvation and vow to live for him our whole lives. People of different religions or no religion can carry out the marriage vows, but they can't take the vows of baptism, and they can't live them out. So I will marry you if you want, but I will not discuss baptizing your baby until we finish that business first."

We argued back and forth, but we weren't getting anywhere. They were agitated, and I was stubborn, so we backed off. I lightened the conversation to something we could agree on. I made my exit.

I was surprised three weeks later when the phone rang and the man asked if I would perform a wedding ceremony for them. Of course I would.

The wedding was an outdoor affair. It was a nice May Saturday morning. The wedding party of about twenty met at a modest hot-springs resort. There we all crammed into a few four-wheel-drive vehicles. We drove thirty minutes up abandoned logging roads, endless hairpin turns, dodging logs and potholes.

The site for the wedding was so beautiful it sucked the air right out of you. We were on a rock ledge, a precipice a thousand feet above Trapper Creek, which cuts its way through the Bitterroot Wilderness down to the Bitterroot River. I looked down at the creek and wondered about the fishing. Directly across Trapper Creek Draw was Trapper Peak, the highest mountain in the Bitterroots. It was so close you felt like you could lick the glacier. Trapper Peak is several sharp pinnacles of granite, points where the secrets of the foundation of the world are lifted up and exposed for everyone to see for miles and miles.

The wedding party was in full formal dress. Family and friends had flown in from all over the country. The mothers negotiated high heels on decomposed granite around a thousand-foot ledge. Even though the service was twenty feet from the edge, we couldn't help but feel the presence of the ledge. The baby was there, of course, and was held by the maid of honor.

I liked the setting, because marriage is life on a rocky ledge. There is danger involved. It is exceptionally beautiful. But there is no beauty without danger, no gain without risk. The great views in life are always from its precipices. I was proud to help this young couple take the risk on their own precipice, the risk to become something beautiful.

As we gathered there, Trapper Peak stood behind us, exposing its bedrock to the world. At the same time the bride and groom stood there, exposed bedrock too. Marriage is the foundational institution of the human race. Man and woman's becoming inseparable flesh is an inseparable part of what it means to be human.

The party at Medicine Hot Springs was great. Good food and dancing: a time of celebration. At the reception the bride's mother handed me an envelope, saying: "This is for your good works, Father." I stuffed it in my suit coat.

The bride's father was a glum fellow. He looked as if he had the weight of the world in his bowels. I take such people as a challenge, so I sat beside him and poked around a little bit. Saying "hi" and "isn't it a nice day" didn't get me very far, but I noticed that he was wearing a cap with the name of a gigantic computer corporation embossed on the front.

"You work for that company?"

"Yes."

"What do you do for 'em?"

"I'm the chief executive officer," he said, sober as a Puritan.

"Just workin' your way up the ladder, huh?" I responded with a smirk.

He suffered himself a smile, and then figured what the heck and just cut loose laughing. We had a great time after that, talking about mainframe computers, which I knew nothing about, and he knew it, and I knew he knew it, but neither of us cared.

After the party, as soon as I'd driven out of sight, I opened the envelope to see how much my good works were worth. Two hundred and fifty bucks. Our Chevy desperately needed four new tires.

Dust

The voice on the phone sounded young and drunk. His speech was slurred and uncertain.

"Are you the preacher?"

I responded with a reluctant yes.

"How do you do a funeral?" he asked.

"What do you want?"

"My brother died. We need a funeral for him, down at the river."

It made sense now. Of course I would help. I got directions to the house and drove over.

The rusted trailer house had a porch added. The yard was littered with old refrigerators, car bodies and tires. The father answered the door. His face was thick, fleshy and red. His eyes were sad and wet.

It was summer and hot, so we sat on the porch and visited.

"Charley wasn't a bad boy," he began. "He just got into some trouble."

"How did he die?" I asked.

"He was riding his motorcycle down the railroad tracks . . . he lost control and slammed into a bridge abutment."

I couldn't help asking him the obvious next question. "What was he doing riding a motorcycle on railroad tracks?"

"He was being chased by the police."

The tone of his answer suggested that our discussion of Charley's life and death was now over, and I was more than happy to oblige. I didn't need to know a lot about him.

We went on to discuss the details of the funeral. It was to be a simple service at a park on the river.

I knew it would be informal, so I wore blue jeans and a sport shirt. I was overdressed.

The congregation that gathered at the park by the river consisted of a few older folks, friends of the parents, and about forty people Charley's age. I knew the family wasn't at the top of the Bitterroot social ladder, but I wasn't prepared for a motorcycle gang. There must have been twenty Harleys. The men and women wore mostly dust-impregnated denim and black leather. Their boots bristled with spikes. Tattoos were part of the uniform. There were some kids there too.

I spoke to the brother a little before the service. He explained the choice of the park: "Yeah, we wanted to have it down here at the river 'cause when we were kids this is where we partied."

It was August, and the bare dirt around the picnic tables had been ground by the crowds to a deep, fine dust. We stood in the dust and gathered around a picture of Charley that had been set up on a picnic table. The river ran quietly behind us.

I stood up and called them to attention. Before introducing myself, I stopped for a moment and looked into the eyes of the people in the congregation. Their eyes were deeply empty. At rich people's funerals the eyes are sometimes shallow, choked with avarice and defensiveness. Here there was nothing to lose. I saw deep loss, abyss.

During the opening prayer Charley's mother fainted. We stopped the service while she was revived and propped up in a lawn chair. During her revival I again observed the congregation. A man stood aside from the rest, leaning against a tree. He wore nothing but blue jeans and boots. His bare brown chest was covered with tattoos. His clean chestnut hair hung to the middle of his back. His eyes were shiny coal-black and sharp as pencil points. He was quiet, stoned and angry.

I could not meet this need. Jesus needed to be the minister today. I decided to introduce them to Christ and let him wander around taking their sins away. He would bear their burden, if only I could bear him to them.

After some readings and a few words about Charley, I knew what I had to do, and I was eager for the opportunity.

"This afternoon I would like to tell you about Jesus Christ. Jesus was a carpenter, which in ancient times meant that he was a car mechanic. If your cart broke down you brought it to Jesus. Jesus was a regular guy . . ."

Quietly but firmly, with the love of the Spirit, I told them the gospel story. I talked about Jesus' work as a carpenter, his teachings, his miracles, his rejection by religious and political authorities, his death for the forgiveness of sins, his resurrection for eternal life, his presence here now and our need to accept him. No bells or whistles, just straight, simple gospel.

They listened very carefully. I was taking them seriously, and they took me seriously. And then,

Earth to earth, ashes to ashes, dust to dust. Glory be to the Father and to the Son and to the Holy Ghost. As it was in the beginning, is now and ever shall be, world without end. Amen.

Afterward a few of them expressed appreciation. Charley's brother came up and said, "I'll get you later for this."

I didn't know what he meant. It kind of scared me.

Three weeks later he came to my door with his hand held out like he had a gun. He smiled and handed me a twenty-dollar bill.

Six months later I did his funeral at the river.

Bread and Blood

"Our hymn of gathering this morning before the celebration of the Lord's Supper is number 326, 'All Hail the Power of Jesus' Name.' During the final stanza, will the servers please come forward."

I don't pay much attention to the tune the accompanist is playing. I light out loudly singing one of my favorite hymns to the tune "Coronation." I am blundering forward, imagining myself leading the congregation, when about halfway through the first verse I realize that everyone is singing a different tune. I stop the hymn. I turn red.

"Are we singing the same hymn tune?" I ask the congregation and the accompanist.

We all laugh.

"No," the accompanist replies. She continues gently: "There are three tunes to this hymn. The bulletin says number 326, and you are singing the hymn tune on page 325."

"Oops—well, let's sing number 325; that's the one I meant."

The accompanist fires up "Coronation," and with my pride slightly bruised, we sing the hymn. During the last stanza a thought hits me.

I move from the pulpit to behind the table. I look the people in their eyes and say: "I want you to know that singing the wrong hymn tune was my mistake, not the accompanist's. And it was just a mistake. That's OK, we all make mistakes, and we admit them, brush them off and go on. But that is not what this table is about.

"Jesus didn't die for our imperfections. He didn't die for our mistakes.

God brushes off our mistakes and imperfections just like we do, even more easily, in fact. No, this meal which brings us the death of Jesus is for our sin.

"*Sin is not a mistake.* Our sin is our willing unlawfulness, our purposeful breaking of God's law. In attitude and in deed, we rebel against God, and we have for that reason forfeited our right to live. We deserve to die for our sins. That's what the death of Jesus is for. For our deliberate unlawfulness.

"We all make mistakes, and we can all brush them off. But our dilemma caused by our offense against God, the removal of the penalty we deserve, can only be solved by the act of God. God must provide the solution.

"The act of God where our rebellion against God is taken care of and we are given new life is contained right here in the broken body and shed blood of our Savior. Jesus didn't die for your mistakes, he died for your sin. So right now, bring your sins to Jesus, and he will bring his healing to you."

I pass the bread to the servers; they pass them to the people. I lift a loaf of bread and break it: "On the night on which he was betrayed . . ."

We partake, and I look down at the little cups filled with grape juice. Though I've been a Baptist a long time, after the Episcopalian chalice of my youth filled with gullet-warming wine, these trays of plastic cups still look silly to me. But then I look into the cups and I see the blood. God is listening: time to pray.

"Let us pray.

"Lord, the world takes the pretty symbols of Christianity and uses them for their own purposes. But Lord, we choose the unpretty symbols. We choose the blood. Lord, we rejoice in the blood of Jesus. The blood of the Son of God shed for the forgiveness of our sins. Cover us with the blood, cleanse us with the blood, purify us with the blood. Make us new with the blood of Jesus. Make us mindful of its cost, and work its forgiving miracle deeply in us, that we would be free from guilt and ready for the new possibilities for life that forgiveness brings to us. In the name of Jesus we pray, amen."

I pass the blood of Christ to the servers, and we celebrate our life in Christ. Afterward we sing a hymn, "Guide Me, O Thou Great Jehovah." I check quickly. Thankfully, there's only one tune.

God's love is not a theory, nor does it meet an abstract need. God's love is a factual, historic action: the death of Jesus Christ. The purpose of God's act of love is to meet our real need, the forgiveness of our sins.

As I visit with people, I meet over and over the need for the forgiveness of sins. The answer isn't "counseling" people that they never sinned, or that their sin isn't a big deal. The answer is God's solution: sin is a big deal, and the death of Jesus Christ is God's response.

Nothing delivers the death of Jesus like the Lord's Supper. The Lord's Supper takes people seriously. It meets their need with a solution adequate in scope to their sin: God's righteousness. You cannot relieve real sin with a theory or a theology. It takes a real solution in a form as concrete as the sin itself. In delivering the death of Jesus, the Lord's Supper delivers the actual experience of the forgiveness of sins.

People are freed for new life—new life with God and new life with each other. The Table is a feast. It is a celebration of our life together founded on God's work in Christ. We gather as a community broken by our sin and leave as a community healed by God's forgiveness.

It doesn't matter to me if the Lord's Supper is an ordinance, a sacrament, a symbol or the literal transubstantiation of Jesus Christ. It isn't my job to figure this out any more than it is the physician's responsibility to know the precise chemical composition of an antibiotic. My responsibility is to diagnose the problem, choose the medicine and administer it. The problem is sin, the medicine is the death of Jesus, and I poke the needle: the Lord's Supper.

X

Leadership

He calls his own sheep by name
and leads them out.

J O H N 1 0 : 3

My two-point parish presented me with a unique leadership challenge. Everything was in twos. I served two churches (from here on referred to as Church A and Church B). The parish cooperated with two denominations, the Presbyterian Church (U.S.A.) and the American Baptist Churches U.S.A. This in and of itself meant two forms of baptism, two types of church polity, two sets of conventions and committees, and of course two sets of denominational junk mail. The churches were in different towns. The towns were in different counties, so I had two ministerial groups. The churches were not even in the same telephone exchange, so one was long distance from my home.

Needless to say, with two churches I had two councils and two sets of church committees. The churches both worshiped on Sunday morning, one at 9:15 and the other at 11:00. My week was split in half, with two days of office hours in each church.

With two of everything, I could only do what I really needed to do.

I had time to prepare sermons and preach. I had time to pray. I had time to befriend people. I had time to lead Bible studies. I had time to do weddings and funerals. I had time to attend the council meetings and a few committee meetings. I had time to go fishing. So I just did those things.

I'd go to denominational meetings and hear of their newest programs for evangelism, stewardship, training the laity and on and on. I'd go away depressed because I didn't have time to try any of them. Now I'm glad I didn't. We never had an evangelism program, but the people in the churches were doing evangelism all the time. We never had a stewardship drive, but both churches became financially stable. We never trained people how to call, but on hospital calls I was usually the second or third person from the church who'd been there.

My two churches were very different. I knew that I could not and should not force them into a similar mold. I knew my leadership role was to let Jesus Christ lead the churches. So I tried to free them to grow differently.

Church A had a person willing to do youth work, a woman with some small children and a supportive husband. I didn't help her much. We met once in a while to go over things. With prayer, hard work and love she built the best youth group I've ever seen in any church of any size.

Small schools don't offer many peer options. When she started, our kids didn't have a lot of choices; they had to be part of the drinking/drugtaking crowd or have no friends at all. (The motorcycle gangs made sure our little towns were well stocked with big-city drugs.)

The youth leader single-handedly gave the town's youth an option. In so doing, she literally changed the town. Eventually she saw almost 20 percent of the public high school attend her youth group.

Church B, on the other hand, had no youth program at all, and the church and the town suffered as a result. We just didn't have a leader for it.

But Church B had great love feasts. Its potlucks were koinonia celebrations and healing services. Sometimes during a dinner I'd just stand off to the side and watch the people minister to each other. People didn't just sit with their friends. Old people were visiting with young people. New people were never alone. I could see people with problems visiting with people who desired to help them. It was no big deal, they just shared their lives with one another and laughed. Laughter was everywhere. People told stories. Fishermen lied to anyone gullible enough to listen. I know that people met Jesus at these potlucks. We just got together and let people visit.

In Church A, unless there was a special program, we'd plan a potluck and a handful would show. We'd sit around and look at each other, embarrassed. By the end of my tenure we didn't have many potlucks. Nobody would come.

Church A had a spectacular choir. Church B had no choir. We couldn't pull it off. Church A's worship was liturgical and formal, while Church B's worship was very informal. At Church A we asked the congregation not to applaud for the choir or special music. At Church B we never stopped it. Church A said "trespasses." Church B said "debtors." In Church A we celebrated the Lord's Supper once a month. In Church B (the less liturgical!) we celebrated the Lord's Supper twice a month.

Community Leader

I didn't attend a single high-school football or basketball game in either town during my first eight years. I attended a few in my last year, because my children were in the pep band. I was never in the PTA or in any other parent group. I never attended a civic club meeting in either town. Though invited, I never met with the coffee-klatch boys, never became part of the morning meetings at the local coffee shops where the town fathers, businessmen and ranchers got together to discuss things.

And yet somehow I ended up being a powerful person in each of the towns. When the teachers and the school board were at each other's throats, several times I helped avert strikes. When a bond issue to build needed classrooms and athletic facilities failed twice, on the third and last try I was asked to help. I never said a word about it in church, but I lent my support as a private citizen. The bond passed, and many people, including the school superintendent, said that my support made a big difference.

The other community desperately needed a new senior citizens' center. I was asked to be on the committee to build a new center. I attended a few meetings and then dropped out. They had trouble raising money until someone in our church donated the land. No one asked him to— he just did it. Those of us who cared about the project asked the church council to give a thousand dollars to it. I think those two events, the donation of the land and the thousand-dollar gift, broke the ice. Donations started coming in, and soon the town had the best senior citizen center in the valley. I know our church had a lot to do with the success of the project.

I never wanted to be involved in local politics. And I never liked it when I was asked to help out. Everyone knew that I didn't care about political power, so I guess they trusted my opinion.

One day it just struck me that I was a powerful person in both towns. I'd done nothing to deserve it; I hadn't wanted it; the concept made me very uncomfortable, but it was a fact. I was a leader whether I wanted to be or not. Somehow, as I had gone around just doing my pastoral duties, I had exercised community leadership and become a community leader.

Looking back objectively at twenty years of church work, from youth work to pastoral ministry, I see that some of my best work has been my leadership. But I don't know what I've done, and I don't really know how to be a leader. I often begin a day by saying to myself, "Today I need to prepare a sermon," or "Today I need to go off and pray," but I never start any day by saying, "Today I need to be a leader." I wouldn't know what to do if I were trying to be a leader. The best I can figure is that leadership is something I do while I am doing everything else.

Leadership in Prayer

I had visions. The visions were mental pictures of my parishioners, of the churches and of the two churches working together as a parish. Each of the pictures was a vision of what the parishioner or church was and what they might become under the lordship of Christ.

On long wandering-prayer walks by the river I saw visions, gentle vision-whispers about the church. Normally I sloughed them off and tried to "go back to prayer," thinking that the vision meant my mind was wandering. Later I'd find myself telling someone something I saw while my mind was "wandering." My visions became the stock of my pastoral conversations; they become the vocabulary bank, the story bank, the reservoir from which my pastoral conversations and all my pastoral work came.

God redrew the pictures as I walked and prayed. During my prayer for people, the pictures changed. My goal was to avoid superimposing my pictures over God's visions. This is one of the most practical ways that I worked to keep Christ Lord of the churches; I kept him Lord of my visions of the churches. Much of my pastoral leadership amounted to simply going around telling people the pictures I saw. I never told them how we were going to get there, or when. I just told them the pictures and left it at that. I never announced to anyone that I had visions. I never had to. Visions have their own authority. True visions from God don't need to be pushed or coerced into reality. They have their own power. They just need to be shared.

Sitting over coffee on cold December days, I'd swap stories with a parishioner. When I ran into a friend at the grocery store, we'd stop in the aisle for a moment and allow our lives to intersect, with laughs and aphorisms. At a church workday, painting side by side, a parishioner and I would talk about our lives. I'd tell people about the pictures. Sometimes when I told people the pictures I saw, they saw the pictures too, and they began to see themselves in them.

Sometimes the visions came true. People would come to me out of the blue and say they wanted to start something new in the church. They didn't know where the idea had come from, and I didn't either, but it was amazing how often the ideas fit into my vision for the church. The people took the visions of the church I gave them and drew themselves into the visions. Out of this process came many ideas for ministries and growth that I could never have come up with myself. Because of this I didn't have to spend much time coercing people to staff the programs of my visions. Since the people saw the visions themselves, and since they saw themselves in the visions, they were happy to work.

Every time I *tried* to make my visions come true, everything fell flat. Much of my pain as a leader came from trying to force my own visions into flesh.

I wanted a computer to help me with my work. I could see a portable computer helping me handle the problems of having two offices and no secretary. I saw the vision, and I became fixed on my vision. I wanted it my way. I knew how the board would handle my vision. They'd "mickey-mouse" around with it forever. They'd study it ad nauseam. Of course, their method of mickey-mousing around with things built a beautiful new sanctuary, but I wanted my computer now, and I wanted it my way.

I called a special parish board meeting on a snowy January night, rammed the idea down their throats and demanded a vote right then and there. The vote was split, six to five in favor of getting the computer. There were hard feelings over that vote for years afterward. If I'd waited for the idea to take hold the right way, I wouldn't have hurt the feelings of some people who were very dear to me, and I might have ended up with a better computer than the one I got.

When I am at the center of my own visions, Jesus isn't leading the church. In long, wandering prayer I struggled with my visions until Jesus was in the center of the vision and I was at the periphery.

When I present visions in which my ideas, my work, my experiences, my expertise, my gain, my career and my leadership are front and center, I am well on the way to becoming a religious despot. As P. T. Forsyth says, "The ideal minister is three things at least. He is a prophet, and he is a pastor, but he is just as much priest. What he is not is a king."[1]

Leadership in Preaching

I keep my visions out of my sermons. My ideas for the church, even those inspired by the Holy Spirit, have no place in the pulpit; they are not the material of proclamation. Jesus Christ is the object of proclamation. Preaching our visions and ideas for the church is cheap leadership, and it is not preaching. But biblical, Christocentric preaching is powerful pastoral leadership. One can administrate church programs without preaching, but it is doubtful if a pastor can effectively lead the church without preaching. How can this be?

"Man does not live on bread alone, but on every word that comes from the mouth of God," Jesus said, quoting Deuteronomy 8:3. The proclamation of the Word of God is the food of the people of God, nourishing body, soul and spirit. A good sermon is like the breakfast the risen Jesus prepared for his bone-weary disciples, fish cooking on coals, and bread.

Preaching Christ fulfills the cry of the prophet:
Come, all you who are thirsty,
    come to the waters;
and you who have no money,
    come, buy and eat!
Come, buy wine and milk
    without money and without cost.
Why spend money on what is not bread,
    and your labor on what does not satisfy?
Listen, listen to me, and eat what is good,
    and your soul will delight in the richest of fare. (Is 55:1-2)

Preaching Christ is the richest fare. "He has taken me to the banquet hall, and his banner over me is love" (Song 2:4).

Preaching clever ideas, church programs, politics and heartwarming stories is thin soup. But bringing the Word of God faithfully to people week after week is a gourmet feast, good to taste and good for the soul. Christians who hear good preaching learn to "taste and see that the LORD is good" (Ps 34:8). They develop a taste for the Word. They love to hear the Word of God, thoughtfully prepared, lovingly presented.

Jesus tells us that the sheep follow the shepherd:

The man who enters by the gate is the shepherd of his sheep. The watchman opens the gate for him, and the sheep listen to his voice. He calls his own sheep by name and leads them out. When he has brought out all his own, he goes on ahead of them, and his sheep follow him because they know his voice. But they will never follow a stranger; in fact, they will run away from him because they do not recognize a stranger's voice. (Jn 10:2-5)

Now to be honest, Jesus is not being terribly original here. Any farm boy can tell you that sheep will always follow the shepherd, and that cattle will always crowd around the cowboy that feeds them. Of course they don't follow the stranger; why should they? They do not recognize the stranger's voice, because it is not the voice of the one who feeds them.

The people of God will follow the pastor who feeds them the Word of God. That isn't to say that they won't balk once in a while. They can make the pastor's life a living hell. But week in and week out, year in and year out, Christians will not cut themselves off from the one who sets their spiritual table. Even the delinquent son has an uncanny sense of when dinner's on, and he knows he will not be refused.

While the people of God want desperately to flock to the spiritual food of the Word of God, pastors flock to seminars on how to run church boards, administrate programs and raise up volunteers. They come home with straw to feed their people. Then they wonder why their parishioners are not energized by their new social-scientifically correct leadership methods for manipulating them. Cows don't like being herded into vaccination chutes. People don't either.

Good alfalfa hay, cut just before the blossoms open and well cured in the hot sun, can have over 20 percent protein content. Cows can make steak out of hay because good hay is very high in protein. But not all hay is good hay. Poor hay may have half as much protein as good hay. The growth and health of the animal are in direct proportion to the quality of the feed.

It may sound crass to compare the growth of a cow with the growth of Christians, but the fact is, Christians grow and are healthy in direct proportion to the quality of the preaching they feed on. Healthy, growing Christians are happy to volunteer for things, and they give their financial support. Nothing increases offerings better than good preaching. People give to perceived value. Instead of working at raising the offerings, we should work at raising the value of what our parishioners receive from the pulpit.

Leadership is not seeking compliance from our people; it is, more than anything, demanding competence from ourselves. Easy preaching makes leadership hard; hard preaching makes leadership easy.

But there is more to the importance of preaching for pastoral leadership than feeding people the Word of God. When Christ is preached, heard and believed, he becomes Lord in the lives of those who receive him, and he becomes Lord in the church that corporately hears and believes. The goal of parenting is for the child to follow God. The goal of preaching is for the parishioner to follow Christ. The church must be mastered by Christ from the pulpit.

"He calls his own sheep by name and leads them out. When he has brought out all his own, he goes on ahead of them, and his sheep follow him because they know his voice." How does this happen? How does Christ actually call his people today? No doubt there are many ways, but there is no getting around the fact that first and foremost the people of God are addressed directly by Christ in the preaching of the Word. This becomes clear when we realize that preaching is not sharing our thoughts or telling the people of God how they ought to live. Preaching is not just another mode of human communication at our disposal for leading our people. As Dietrich Bonhoeffer says, "Therefore the proclaimed word is not a medium of expression for something else, something which lies behind it, but rather it is the Christ himself walking through the congregation as the Word."[2] The congregation of God's people hear the voice of Jesus in the preaching of Christ.

Those who hear Christ call them in a text like Mark 8:34, "If anyone would come after me, he must deny himself and take up his cross and follow me," or in a text like Matthew 7:13, "Enter through the narrow gate. For wide is the gate and broad is the road that leads to destruction, and many enter through it," have questions about what it means for them to deny themselves. They want to know specifically what their cross is, and how they should pick it up. They want to know what the narrow gate is, and how to distinguish the narrow gate in their life from the many wide gates and broad roads before them. This is the role of spiritual direction.

Leadership in Friendship: Spiritual Direction

In my pastoral friendships I do spiritual direction.[3] Spiritual direction is a friendship around spiritual matters which is mutual in love but single-directional in its focus upon the spiritual walk of one of the parties. As a spiritual director, I am the one who listens, paying attention for the work of God in that person's life, and then I point to it.

The difference between spiritual direction and evangelism is that in evangelism my goal is to *give* a testimony, while in spiritual direction my goal is to *hear* a testimony. In evangelism I pray for the opportunity to share the good news, while in spiritual direction I try to help the person understand what happened when he or she received the good news, and what the good news means in his or her life now. Spiritual direction is not an attempt to find faith or create faith; it is an attempt to understand faith. Spiritual direction is faith seeking understanding.

But it is faith seeking understanding in the most specific and personal sense. Spiritual direction is not jawing about theology. It is not a discussion about a theological object of faith. It is an intense search in a specific person's life for the Living Subject of faith already at work—looking for that work, pointing to that work so that the directee can participate in God's work, so that he or she can live in active covenant with God in everyday life.

Most Christians like to theologize. Almost any Christian will be happy to give an opinion of what Jesus meant when he said, "Enter through the narrow gate." Far fewer will come and ask what it means specifically for them to enter through the narrow gate.

The difference between an abstract theological discussion with a parishioner and spiritual direction is like the difference between talking about fishing and going fishing. I hasten to add that there is nothing wrong with talking about fishing! But it sure doesn't take long to sort out the people who just like to talk about fishing from those who really fish. Some people don't like getting wet. Nor does it take long in a theological discussion to discern if people just like to talk theology or if they desperately wish to live theologically.

In any case, the best possible analogy to a spiritual director is a fishing guide. The best fishing guides and the best spiritual directors have a lot in common.

It goes without saying that a fishing guide needs to know the skills of fly fishing and needs to know *how to teach* the skills of fly fishing. A client may know a lot about fly choice, casting, line mending and reading the water; the client may well be another fishing guide! In fact, I've learned that the best fishing guides allow themselves to be guided by another fishing guide on occasion, to learn new skills and new water and to break out of ruts. Or the client may know almost nothing about fly fishing. In either case, all through the process of guiding, the fishing guide is teaching.

Likewise, it goes without saying that spiritual directors need to know the basic skills of prayer, meditation and listening to God, and they need to be able to teach these skills.

The fishing guide needs to be able to focus simultaneously on two objects: the client and the water. Clients don't know where the fish are on the stream (or they wouldn't need a guide), and they almost always have a hard time seeing the fish, even if the trout are rising. The fishing guide looks for the fish and points the fish out to the client, all the while giving close attention to the client's manner of fishing. The guide watches the client's casting, making comments here and there, reading the client as he reads the water. That is the only way he makes the two connect: the strike, the fight, the catch! Because of this, the cardinal rule of guiding is that the fishing guide does not fish during the trip. The guide gives absolute, undivided attention to the client and the water.

In the same way, the spiritual director must stay focused on the directee and on God. The director is not there to learn in conjunction with the directee. The spiritual director does not fish for personal Leviathans while directing. The spiritual director listens to the directee and listens for God. When the director spots God's work, he or she bids the directee cast to the side of the boat where God is. The haul is usually quite great.

The problem at the beginning of direction is the empty net, while the problem by the end of direction is having the strength to pull the net-busting fish on board.

I've fished with a number of guides over the years, and I've had a number of spiritual directors. The very best quality of the very best fishing guides is the very best quality of the very best spiritual directors. The very best fishing guides, the top of the heap of that profession, *all love to watch clients catch fish as much as they like catching fish themselves.* It gets to the point of silliness sometimes the way a truly great fishing guide starts to laugh, even giggle like a grade-school girl, when a client starts catching fish. Likewise, the characteristic that sets the great spiritual directors apart is childlike joy. Out of pure love they give you their undivided attention, and when you catch your fish, when your net is full, there's always that smile, that glint in their eye that tells you they've just spent the best hour of their day with you.

Make no mistake, this is the joy of the Lord. Parabolically, in the director's joy Jesus becomes present. After the two of you have spent an hour or two searching for Jesus, Jesus shows up in full glory, full joy, full love.

Leadership in Sacramental Ministry

Whereas the sermon divides the church into individuals, the sacraments unite individuals with the body of Christ. The preaching of the New Testament divided crowds up, addressed people as individuals and forced them to make decisions. The preaching of John the Baptist was aimed directly at the false security of a supposed familial solidarity with Abraham as counting for something before God. John preached repentance that forced people to make a moral and spiritual choice about the coming kingdom of God. Though they could only decide as individuals, their decision did not leave them rootless, unconnected creatures. Their choice to repent was sealed with a baptism for repentance that resecured them into the new movement of the Spirit of God.

Jesus' Sermon on the Mount is nothing like Joshua's covenant renewal ceremony at Shechem, in which Joshua addressed all of Israel with the demand of the covenant and asked the nation to respond in kind as families and tribes. Jesus ends the Sermon on the Mount with the frank parable of the wise and foolish builders, which says that some will hear his words and put them into practice and others will not. Everywhere he went, Jesus saw some listeners follow and others turn away. Two sisters responded differently to him. When called by his own mother and his brothers, Jesus answered, "Whoever does the will of my Father in heaven is my brother and sister and mother" (Mt 12:50).

The apostle Paul, in the testimony of Acts and in the testimony of his own epistles, caused division and crisis wherever he went. Luke ends Acts saying that through his discussion with the Jews, "some were convinced by what he said, but others would not believe" (Acts 28:24).

No one divided a crowd up more vigorously or more violently than Paul did! And yet Paul is the one who tells us, "You are all sons of God through faith in Christ Jesus, for all of you who were *baptized* into Christ have clothed yourselves with Christ. There is neither Jew nor Greek, slave nor free, male nor female, for you are all one in Christ Jesus" (Gal 3:26-28).

Paul, who gave us the vision of the church as the body of Christ, tells us how we are incorporated into the unity of God's people: "The body is a unit, though it is made up of many parts; and though all its parts are many, they form one body. So it is with Christ. For we were all *baptized* by one Spirit into one body—whether Jews or Greeks, slave or free—and we were all given the one Spirit to drink" (1 Cor 12:12-13).

And finally, Paul cites the Lord's Supper as not merely a sign of our inclusion into Christ, but as our actual participation in the Risen Christ!

Is not the cup of thanksgiving for which we give thanks a participation in the blood of Christ? And is not the bread that we break a participation in the body of Christ? Because there is one loaf, we, who are many, are one body, for we all partake of the one loaf. (1 Cor 10:16-17)

This tension in the life and ministry of Paul between the division preaching creates and the unity the sacraments create has played itself out in Christian history. It is a simple insight that the traditions of Christianity that place heavy stress on the sacraments tend to view individuals from the perspective of the unity of the church, while the traditions of Christianity that place heavy stress on preaching tend to view the church as a collection of individual disciples. Furthermore, traditions that tend toward sacramentalism usually have connectional polity, and traditions that tend toward proclamation tend toward congregational polity. Traditions that stress the unity of the church practice infant baptism; traditions that stress individualism practice believer's baptism.

That being said, it is no coincidence that our practice and theology of the sacraments divide us as Christians, because it is their intended function to unite us: "one Lord, one faith, one baptism" (Eph 4:5).

I said earlier that my ministry was divided into twos—two churches, two denominations, two counties—but the churches were divided within themselves too. Church A was a community church with representations from strongly sacramental and strongly proclamation-oriented traditions; Church B belonged to two denominations, one that tended toward the sacramental and one that tended toward proclamation. The sacramental tradition (an infant baptism tradition) practiced a highly connectional polity, and the proclamation tradition (a believer's baptism tradition) practiced a congregational polity. Both churches struggled for spiritual equilibrium between sacraments and preaching.

This was a happy challenge for me, because with my roots in sacramental *and* proclamation traditions, I could see the need for balance, and I had the personal resources to attempt to provide it. For me it was a blessed opportunity for freedom in pastoral leadership. My strong commitment to preaching had kept me unable to pursue my vocation in sacramental traditions, yet my deep love for the sacraments had made me uncomfortable in many of the churches of the denomination in which I'd been ordained. In the two-church setting I could be as sacramental as I wanted to be and still preach hellfire and brimstone. So I set my course to divide the congregations up into individuals through preaching and to unite the congregations through sacraments.

The pastor leads in administering the sacraments. In all of the different churches and traditions of my experience, from the most sacramental to the least sacramental, there has always been a strong sense, if not a hard-and-fast rule, that the pastor leads at the Lord's Table and the pastor baptizes. Elders and lay ministers assist, but the pastor leads. In all of these churches and traditions, the pastor is usually the one who preaches, but none has a rule that others could not preach. All of these churches encourage the proliferation of lay Bible-study groups, prayer groups, fellowship groups and all kinds of meetings with spiritual talks and sermons. In fact, one sign of strong pastoral leadership is the growth of lay study and prayer groups. But no church or tradition of which I have been a part has ever encouraged small groups within the church to celebrate Communion or practice baptism. Where it is permitted (it is nowhere encouraged), a pastor in the church needs to be present. This instinct is just as prevalent and just as vehement among Baptists as among Episcopalians: anyone can preach, anyone can teach, but the pastor leads the sacraments.

The reason is clear. Preaching and teaching, whose responsibility is to confront us as individuals, are not, if carried out by tested and trusted individuals, a threat to the unity of the church. If our Sunday-school classes are taught by good people, do we fear for the unity of the church? But the sacraments, whose responsibility is to unite us, become a definite threat to the unity of the church if they are celebrated willy-nilly in small groups. Would you allow your Sunday-school teachers, the same ones you trust implicitly to handle the Word of God every Sunday, to celebrate the sacraments in their Sunday-school classes whenever it struck their fancy? Or to baptize a convert on the spot? Absolutely not! To give Sunday-school teachers the freedom to teach is a sign of a pastor's strength as a leader, but to give those same teachers the freedom to baptize and celebrate Communion would be a sign of grave weakness.

There is one exception to the church's discouragement of small groups' celebrating Communion, and this is the practice of shut-in Communion. The practice of this vital and hallowed rite is allowed and encouraged specifically *because of* Communion's characteristic of uniting the church.

I have made many pastoral calls on shut-ins. There are many goals for these calls—to pray for healing, to encourage with Bible reading, to show love. But no pastoral work allows a shut-in to actually experience participation in Christ's body like shut-in Communion.

Baptism and Communion must be celebrated in person; they unite Christians in a concrete way. You can distribute sermons through the mail, either on tape or in manuscript form; you can broadcast sermons and Bible studies over electronic media. But the Lord's Supper can only be distributed person to person, by hand. And you can't mail a baptism. You can only dunk, sprinkle or pour in person.

Leadership in Obeying Our Call: The Last Decision

My hardest leadership task came when it began to dawn on me that it was time for me to leave the parish.

My visions shifted in critical ways. The churches were growing dramatically. Their need for pastoral care was growing too. Meanwhile, I was exhausted. I remember sitting in the stands of our school gym watching my daughter play basketball. I could only stay for the first half, as I had a council meeting to make—the second council meeting of the week. My chest hurt. I had walking pneumonia. Just watching the referees running up and down the court made me short of breath. The crowd razzed them mercilessly, but they were enjoying themselves. I'd never wanted to be a referee, but as I watched them, I began to imagine what it would be like to be able to do something besides work constantly.

My spirit began to long for breathing space. Serving two churches had worn me out. I began to dream about pastoring one church.

I had really believed all along that I would pastor the parish my whole life. That was my goal, anyway. But our two little towns began growing. And the churches began to grow more rapidly. It seemed as if the shift took place over a single night. I just didn't have the time or the energy to pastor the churches anymore. As that dawned on me, it shocked me to see new visions of the churches: I wasn't their pastor anymore; each church had its own pastor. I saw their future, and I wasn't in it.

It's a strange feeling when your call to a church begins to disassemble. There's denial at first. Then sadness. On long walks I told the Lord that I was willing to stay or to leave. Of course there was never any answer. Just visions.

A disturbing vision one day made me face the fact that it was time for me to leave. It came as I was driving on the Florence Bridge over the Bitterroot River. I looked over the edge of the bridge into the water to see if the trout were rising. But my mind jumped to something else. I saw myself relaxed. I felt comfortable. The churches were stagnating, I had cut my work load way down, but nobody cared. I realized that the churches loved me enough that they would let me be their pastor as long as I wanted. So what if I couldn't meet their needs? They'd never fire me.

Two visions competed for my obedience. In one vision the churches were growing and thriving under the leadership of their own pastors. In the other we were all nicely settled into a passive mediocrity. My choices were clear. I could kick back and become a comfortable religious hack. Or I could choose the vision of the churches growing under Christ. I had to choose Christ. My own vision forced me out.

The pain! Toying with dreams of breathing room is one thing, but contemplating the tearful details of leaving people I had given my life to was dreadfully painful.

My last act of pastoral leadership was to preside over my own funeral.[4] I was the body, the undertaker and the preacher. I even had to write my own obituary, my resignation letter.

XI

Leaving

Now I commit you to God
and to the word of his grace . . .

ACTS 20:32

*F*ebruary 12, 1992
From: Pastor David Hansen
To: Members and Friends of the Florence-Victor Parish

Dear Friends in Christ,

I wish I could discuss this issue with each of you face to face, but I am constrained by time to handle this by letter. It is my duty to inform you that I will be resigning my position as pastor of the Florence-Victor Parish, concluding my duties on April 5, 1992. Beginning April 1992 I will be pastor of the Belgrade Community Church, Belgrade, Montana. The church is slightly larger than the Florence-Carlton Community Church, and is a member of the American Baptist Churches, the denomination of my ordination.

Our Life Together

Nine years ago, January 4, 1983, at 4:30 p.m., we drove into Montana in an ice storm. We must have been a pitiful sight. Debbie and I and three small children were stuffed into our Chevy station wagon, behind which we towed our '65 VW Bug. I was a California driver in an ice storm. We were sliding off the crown of the road. We dropped our VW off at the Lozeau Bar just east of Superior and tried to continue, but it didn't help. I didn't know how to drive on ice. We stopped at a rest station a few miles past the Lozeau Bar. It was dark, the kids were crying, Debbie and I were helpless. Just then two construction workers drove into the rest area. They could see our dilemma (we weren't hiding our feelings very well), and they offered to help. They made us an offer: one of them volunteered to drive our station wagon with Debbie and the kids, while I rode in their truck. I was nervous about the situation and felt humiliated. But we were desperate, so we accepted their help. In a couple of hours we were in the IGA parking lot in Florence.

Often our best adventures have difficult beginnings. I was proud of the two churches. They weren't very big, but they'd each survived hard times, and their potential was obvious to me. The Florence church was meeting in their charming but already overcrowded one-hundred-year-old sanctuary. We averaged about seventy-five in worship. The Victor church's building was larger, but in need of repair. We averaged about forty-five per Sunday.

Slowly the churches have grown. Buildings were built and buildings were renovated. Attendance and finances grew, programs expanded, committees popped up like dandelions. Nowadays we are averaging about 220 people on Sunday between the two churches. On February 2, we had 175 in Florence and 110 in Victor—that made the parish a congregation of 285. What each of you sees on Sunday morning is only half of what I see.

Most single churches with attendance of 220 already have or are looking for a full-time associate pastor. Last spring I became aware that pastoring the two churches was becoming physically impossible for me. It was then that it began to dawn on me that my time as pastor of the

Florence-Victor Parish was coming to a close.

Why?

I am weary of serving two churches. I am tired of having two offices, two libraries, two boards and two sets of committees, two denominations, two communities to serve, and the constant driving to keep up with the services, committees and calling. I am tired of being split up into two pieces.

Both churches have been unbelievably tolerant and understanding of my time constraints. You may find this hard to believe, but it is true: in nine years I have not received a single complaint about how much time I spent at one church or the other. This is almost unheard-of in yoked parish ministries. Furthermore, my resignation is not under any kind of outside pressure whatsoever. It has to do with my own exhaustion with my job situation.

I have spent nine years at this job, and now it is time for a change. My family is happy for the change. These nine years have been tiring for them too, though they, like you, have never complained about the situation, not once.

This is a good year for us to move. Evan is entering high school in the fall. (When we came he wasn't even in kindergarten.) Debbie is graduating in June from the University of Montana with her master's degree in school psychology. All of us who know what she's been through over the last years are exceedingly proud of her! She will be living in the Missoula area this spring, commuting to Belgrade for the weekends. She figures this will be her opportunity to experience graduate school "Montana style."

Debbie and I both grew up in families that moved a lot, and we both grew up in big cities. It's hard for us to believe, but we have lived in the Bitterroot Valley longer than either of us had lived anywhere in our whole lives. And of course our children do not remember living anywhere else. This has been a wonderful place for them to have spent their early years. You have been wonderful to our children. All of our children love going to church and Sunday school, because you have cared for them so much over the years. Church is home for them. Thanks.

So now we move to a new town, new home, new schools, new church, even a new side of the continental divide. But new is good. Good for us, and good for you too.

What Next?

We have sixty days to say goodby. That's not much time really, but any more and the pain gets stretched out too long. Also, the churches can't do much in the way of looking for new leadership until I'm gone. Both churches need time to take stock of things. You need to ask questions like, Where do we go from here? What does God want for us now?

I cannot help you do this! When I arrived here in 1983 you had a strong, functioning parish board that through much work, trial and error, faith, common sense, loads of prayer and good advice from denominational leaders made many good decisions about what the churches needed to seek for pastoral leadership. The process was long, but the outcome was good. The process must begin again.

Those of you who have been around a while know that the process works. Those of you who are new need to hang in there and with much prayer follow the lead of those elected as council members to serve the church at this time. Both churches have excellent councils. You can trust them to approach the coming challenges with prayer and genuine concern to seek God's will. In both churches we have found that we can accomplish big projects if we take time, pray and let the ideas percolate all through the congregation. Listening to God together, you can come up with the right decisions.

In the next sixty days the business of the church will go on as usual. I will continue to pour my heart and soul into preaching and teaching the Word of God and into prayer for you.

Saying goodby is part of life, maybe the most important part. It is certainly one of the most difficult things we ever do. I don't imagine this goodby-saying will be easy. But the goal, what we are really looking forward to—and it will come eventually—is the gratitude to God we will feel for the many years we have been granted to be friends in Christ. And that is what you all are to me, dear, dear friends.

Your friend and pastor,
Dave

The Wake

I was dying. I didn't want to face the people. I wanted to put on Frodo's ring and disappear without having to say goodby.

On the first Sunday after the letter, the faces in the pews shot through me like bullets. Some parishioners cried, others were grave, a few were angry. I worked my way through the services in each church step by step, hoping that somehow I could make it through without completely falling apart.

After church in Victor, Earl pulled me aside. Earl was about ninety years old and a dear friend. We'd fished together, lied a lot to each other about fishing; I'd buried his wife of sixty years. We sat in my office on two folding chairs. I was about to break apart. He leaned forward and looked me in the eyes. "Dave, you're doing the right thing," he said.

I sighed. He went on. "You're doing the right thing in leavin', because your work is done here. You came here with a job to do, and you did it, and now it's time for you to move on. No one knows what the future of this church will be after you leave. It may go up, it may go down, it may stay the same. But that is no matter for you to worry about. You've done what you came to do, and now you have to leave. You can't do any more here than you've already done. I respect a man that moves on when his job is done."

I was breathing easier every second. He continued: "Dave, I ushered here over fifty years, and I've never seen this church like it is now. My oh my, before you got here, many times we'd have fifteen people in church and no children at all. And now the church is full. You did what you came to do. You can't do any more than you've already done. The church is full, it's time for you to leave. Oh my, but you've done a good job."

On the drive home from Victor, the tears I'd held in flowed freely. Earl had been sent by God to tell me I was on the right track. Earl was giving me spiritual direction.

There were parties and receptions and thanksgivings. It was all very exhausting. There were hugs and laughter and tears, and they were poignant. I wasn't enjoying it, but I was growing up; I was learning how to say goodby. I was learning how to let something end and let God take over and provide the victory. We all felt that. We all knew that God had worked in our midst and that now he had more work to do and that it didn't include me anymore. Dying like this is letting God have his way.

One afternoon I walked through the new Sunday-school rooms and the new sanctuary. I leaned back in one of the back pews and looked up at the beams. They were massive wooden beams. When the new sanctuary was built, before carpets were down, about five friends and I had climbed up three jacks of scaffolding and stained and varnished all those beams. We'd had fun up there. I was prouder of finishing those beams than of anything else about the new building. They represented all I'd done.

I sat for an hour (or was it two?), and for the first time in nine years I simply savored my accomplishments. I prayed and sang and enjoyed. I'd had a lot of fun over the years. The peace can only be described this way: if I'd have died right then and there, it would have been enough; my life had counted for something. The Lord had established the work of my hands. The beams hung there silent, solid, soaking it in like stain.

The River

There was one last goodby to make. On Wednesday of the last week

I felt a vacuum near my soul. God's ear was ready. I needed to pray. I needed to walk the river for a last time.

Fortunately, the fish were rising and the fishing was good. I caught four nice rainbow trout.

I walked through the scratchy wild roses and the soft grasses, following trails I had made over years of praying trips. I smelled the river. I was alone. The Canada geese were mated up and were securing territory—they honked rudely at me if I crossed their invisible boundaries.

I hung my head and watched my footsteps. I told God about all the things that had happened over the years and that now I was headed to new water. I knew the trail well, I knew the fish well, I knew the river well. All their habits were known to me (and my habits may well have been known to them). My whole ministry had been one long habit of prayer on this river, and now the habit would be broken, until I could find some new water.

But I didn't want to leave my water. I wanted to stay and live here forever. This was my water, these were my fish, this was where I prayed. This was my habit. The river was my best friend.

How can I tell you what it's like to have a river as a best friend? It's always there. Its transparent waters always carry a surprise. Sometimes they yield me fish, sometimes I get skunked. Sometimes a mink will skitter by, or a river otter will hiss at me, or a beaver will slap its tail at me in protest. No matter: through all seasons it accepts my heavy feet, soaks in my talk, and from it my prayer bird takes wing from the wilderness.

The birds were there. Titmice and eagles, geese and meadowlarks, and the ever-present crows, ravens and magpies. My favorite bird in spring is the Eastern kingbird. Kingbirds are small and look insignificant, but they establish territory and jealously protect it against any other bird, including eagles. Kingbirds remind me of pastors protecting their flock from heretics.

The river is a long living parable to me of God's love. It has sustained me during my hardest moments and has rejoiced with me in my victories. My people have been baptized in its water. It has flowed past us into the Clark Fork, into the Columbia and into the Pacific, where it has risen again to cloud over us and wet us again.

When I came to the barbed-wire fence I stopped. This time there was no new water ahead. New water for me is turning back, leaving the river. It was hard to turn back toward home. As long as I was walking upriver, away from my house, I could deny that it was over. Now I knew I had to turn around.

The walk home was slower. My steps were deliberate and heavy. I stumbled a bit as I purposely kicked stumps and downed logs that I'd stepped over a hundred times before: now I had to say goodby to them. Blundering is a polite way of saying goodby to a branch.

The closer I got to the top of the bluff overlooking the river, the harder it got. I kept praying, "New water, new water."

I reached the top of the bluff, a hundred feet above the river, and looked across at it all. Below me was the Bitterroot River, ever moving, ever alive. I raised my gaze directly west across the Bitterroot Valley to the Bitterroot Mountains. They rise high and snow-capped above our valley. I looked up the draw where I got hypothermia, and I laughed. I had beaten death once.

I sucked in as much river air as I could hold and let it out slow. Rivers, like oceans, are graves and wombs. Especially in the spring. Mingled they are sweet, but river smells are smells of death. Dead grasses, dead deer, dead leaves, mixed with water smells and—as the sun beats down on the wet cold earth—life smells from tiny shootlets of grass stemming up through the mud.

I wasn't the only one who'd been here. Lewis and Clark had admired this river. One winter of their journey it saved their lives. Countless others had smelled the smells, caught the trout, heard the wind whish through the ponderosa pines. They were dead now. And I would also die. I sat there, and I was so deeply grateful to God for life—for my opportunity to be alive here and to have known this river, to participate in its habits and to love the people who lived on its banks.

All the gravity of life and death kept me sitting there gazing, praying and thanking, and I didn't want to get up. But I did get up, turned and walked east, and did not turn back for so much as a glance.

XII

Reward

"I tell you the truth," Jesus said to them,
"no one who has left home or wife or brothers or parents
or children for the sake of the kingdom of God
will fail to receive many times as much in this age and,
in the age to come, eternal life."

LUKE 18:29-30

*A*s I entered the birthing room of the hospital, the first thing I saw was her eyes. I wasn't ready for them yet, so I scanned the surroundings.

She was on the bed, in a hospital gown. Nurses were around, her husband was there, she had an IV in her arm pumping in the drug to induce labor. But there was no possible happy ending. We knew that the seven-month-old baby inside her was dead. Today she had to deliver it.

As I walked closer, I felt the power of the Spirit of God's love. My guts shook: *splanchna.* But my blood pressure felt as if it was lowering. Something was telling my body to slow down. Nothing was demanded of me but to be there. I was as important a component of what was happening as the doctors and nurses. But I had nothing to do. My role was to be quiet.

No one told me I was supposed to do this. I didn't know I was supposed to do this. I just entered the room, and as soon as I saw her eyes, I knew that my role today was simply to be the source of the quiet.

Now I could look at her.

I looked into her eyes. As I got close, she reached up for an embrace and I returned it.

I told her: "I love you, dear, and I'm going to be here today."

"Thank you," she said, and her eyes softened.

I don't think I'm the one who said it; I don't think I'm the one she heard say it. I think we both just listened to it and knew who said it.

Now it was just a lot of hard work. The contractions began, and the father and the nurses assisted her as I watched. Later the father and I went out to lunch. We made small talk, but mostly I was quiet. Being quiet was my job that day; so I gave him some of my quietness.

In the afternoon the time came for the delivery. I stepped out. The father, the nurses and the doctor were in the room. Meanwhile, some friends from church had showed up. We sat quietly and prayed.

After about an hour the doctor and the nurses came out, and a nurse asked me to go in the room. They wanted me in the room. I walked in, and there were mother and father, holding the baby. Huddling over the baby's body in awe and anguish. I came up to their side and looked too. Her skin was grayish-green and beginning to blister off. She had Mommy's chin. Her name was Bonnie Jeanne.

Some friends from church came into the room. We all gathered in a circle and held hands for prayer. I prayed:

"O Lord, we worship you. We thank you and praise you, for you are a good and loving God, full of goodness and lovingkindness, which you have shown to us in many ways over many years. We do not understand this event, but we ask your presence and your peace and your healing with us now as we gather at this sad time . . ."

God was there. We all felt God, we all knew God was there, and we all worshiped. Somehow, in the utter absence, with all of our possibilities at an end, our hope used up, when for all practical purposes God had forsaken us all and abandoned us to death along with the child, God was there.

The Reward

Here is the reward of the pastoral ministry: being with people and bringing the love of Christ to them. Being in that birthing room. Just being wanted in that room. Being with the brothers and sisters in Christ, and with them feeling and knowing and experiencing and trusting God's loving presence: that is the reward a pastor receives.

When I leave a church, it doesn't owe me anything. I'm not its employee; it doesn't owe me a gold watch. Looking back, I feel like I owe them. I owe them for giving me the opportunity to be their pastor. They provided for my family's needs so that I could wander around praying, visiting with people, studying the Bible, teaching it and preaching the Word of God. They allowed me to serve them. They allowed me to be with them in the deepest moments of their lives. I have become their friend. I will be friends with that mom and dad for the rest of our lives. We will be friends on a level that is unobtainable to other people— certainly unobtainable to professionals, whether medical or psychological.

Doctors and nurses and therapists and counselors and friends and family and all others do wonderful things and have invaluable roles to play. But I'm the only one who brings God. I bring God by doing nothing technologically or professionally significant at all.

I was just there. The technological and professional people were at the end of their resources. The baby was dead. All they could do was mop up. But God wasn't done. We didn't know what he was doing. I didn't try to speak for him. It wasn't my responsibility to say what he was doing. It was my responsibility to bring him and let him work. That's why I had nothing to do. That's why I had to be quiet. I had to be quiet so that God could be there in that inscrutable place of absolute absence of anything godly at all.

When you do that for people, when you show up and when God shows up because you are there, and God heals in the most impossible places, that person's soul is forever linked with yours in a way that extends from this life into eternal life. It's love that has the scent of eternity to it. Somehow in that birthing room it was impossible not to believe in eternal life. It was quite literally impossible not to believe in God.

When you are with people at times like that, when together you experience God's presence so powerfully that it is impossible not to believe in him, your souls become bound in a depth experience that changes you all, forever. You become integrally grateful to these people. The gratitude comes out of the historical fact that our spiritual existence has emerged from what we have experienced together. We become brothers and sisters because our souls are forged together within the same womb and we emerge from the same womb of suffering. That's why pastors have so many brothers and sisters in so many places. By definition, brothers and sisters come out of the same womb. We have gone into death with people, into the valley of the shadow of death with many people, and through Christ we have emerged whole, new people. These people are our brothers and sisters now, and they will be forever.

I believe strongly that we take these memories into heaven. Not the memories of the delivery of a dead baby—after all, we will be with Bonnie Jeanne alive in heaven—but there will be a soul memory, a soul gratitude, a soul thanksgiving for one another. These memories, these relationships, all these brothers and sisters are the "treasures in heaven" Jesus refers to. Pastors will be rewarded with innumerable such treasures.

We don't take our heavenly reward seriously enough. We do have a heavenly reward that is special, splendid. Unfortunately, our view of heaven is so egalitarian that we have reduced our lives to a meaningless wait here for nothing special there. This is not right.

Remarking on Jesus' promise of reward and retribution as motive for moral living, New Testament scholar Leonhard Goppelt says,

Such discourses on reward and retribution seem strange because the view expressed in philosophy from Plato to Kant has been that righteousness bears its reward in itself and that goodness must be practiced for its own sake. Behind such thinking is the concept of human autonomy. One lives by a general moral code or an ethical principle in order to realize oneself by doing so. For Biblical thought, this autonomy based on itself was self-deception.[1]

People today are living for themselves and for their own achievements. They live as their own end. The self-made man and the self-made woman of today are unashamedly their own eschaton. How can they help but look at life this way when the god they believe in neither rewards good nor condemns evil?

It's just plain true that the more our world values autonomy and self-realization, the more discouraged and defeated we pastors have become. The more the world around us becomes its own eschaton, the less we will be understood and appreciated for what we do. And to the extent that we pastors accept the world's stance and attempt to become our own destinies through autonomy, the more we will despise our call and demand satisfaction now for our efforts. That's when we start trying to make stones into bread.

We need to face the fact that in a world where people invent and reward themselves, we pastors can never count for much. In this world we can never be important professionally. Most of our parishioners don't know what we do. Many of them wonder if what we do is worth a whole lot. Even we aren't sure if what we do amounts to a hill of beans.

But this world is passing. The world of self-made men and women is passing away at this very moment. We get little tastes of how this world is passing away and of what the new world God is bringing will be.

That birthing room was filled with professionals. The doctors and nurses were professionals, the parents were professionals in their work, the church friends who came were professionals. But really there were no professionals there at all. There were no self-made men or women in that room. There was no one in that room with any human ability to do anything significant to change what was happening. The only one who could bring anything to the situation to redeem any part of that world was God. God was there, God was all in all there, and we were all in God there. At that spot in our pilgrimage God gave us a hint of our ultimate reward.

God said to his greatest pilgrim and the father of all who believe, "Do not be afraid, Abram. I am your shield, your very great reward" (Gen 15:1).

God is our reward. Crying out in the wilderness, we taste our tears and lick resurrection life. We taste eternal life in a living parable. We are encountered by God in a person who is called by God, formed by God and empowered by God to do absolutely nothing but be there in his name. The metaphor comes and goes, but the effect remains. The issue of the pastoral ministry is solved: *God exists, and he exists for us in Jesus Christ.* There is no other issue for pastoral ministry, no other question to be answered. Job's answer suffices for us: "I know that my Redeemer lives, and that in the end he will stand upon the earth. And after my skin has been destroyed, yet in my flesh I will see God" (Job 19:25-26). Job lacked one thing: he never had a pastor.

And when I think that God was in that hospital Job-room partly because I was there—not because of anything I did or said, but merely because I showed up and stood there with that mother and father—I can't imagine doing anything else my whole life but be a pastor.

Notes

Chapter 1: Beginning
[1]Eberhard Jüngel, *God as the Mystery of the World*, trans. Darrell L. Guder (Grand Rapids, Mich.: Eerdmans, 1983), p. 289.
[2]Ibid.

Chapter 2: Call
[1]Bob and Rosie Cahill. Through their ministry in several small Baptist churches, some two dozen young men and women have entered theological seminary.
[2]This is a favorite aphorism of Robert Cahill.
[3]P. T. Forsyth, "The Ideal Ministry," *The British Congregationalist*, October 18, 1906; quoted in *Revelation Old and New*, ed. John Huxtable (London: Independent Press, 1962), p. 110.
[4]John W. Doberstein, ed., *Minister's Prayer Book* (Philadelphia: Fortress, 1968), p. 198.

Chapter 3: The Holy Spirit
[1]Dietrich Bonhoeffer in *Psalms: The Prayer Book of the Bible* (Minneapolis: Augsburg, 1970), pp. 64-65.

Chapter 4: Temptation
[1]These three particular roles, entertainer, counselor and manager, are my adaptation of the three characters, the Rich Aesthete, the Manager and the Therapist, that Alasdair MacIntyre talks about in his wonderful book *After Virtue*, 2nd ed. (Notre Dame, Ind.: University of Notre Dame Press, 1984), pp. 28-30. MacIntyre says these three roles characterize our society's values and are valued highly because of their manipulative functions. It is not coincidental that pastors are lured away from prayer, Bible teaching and loving pastoral care into these activities.

Chapter 5: Eschatology
[1]C. K. Barrett, *Romans* (New York: Harper & Row, 1957), p. 227; Ernst Käsemann, *Commentary on Romans*, trans. and ed. Geoffrey W. Bromiley (Grand Rapids, Mich.: Eerdmans, 1980), p. 157; Karl Barth, *The Epistle to the Romans* (Oxford, U.K.: Oxford University Press, 1933), p. 182.
[2]Barth, *Epistle to the Romans*, p. 182.
[3]E. P. Sanders, *Paul and Palestinian Judaism* (Philadelphia: Fortress, 1977), p. 473.
[4]In the fall of 1985 in Spokane, Washington, I had the privilege of visiting privately with Eberhard Busch, Barth's last assistant and author of the biography *Karl Barth*. Among other things we discussed Karl Barth and universalism; Busch affirmed Barth's consistent denial of universalism but also his explicit openness to the possibility of it, saying that his answer to the question of universalism was

simply "Why not?"

⁵J. S. Whale, *Christian Doctrine* (Cambridge, U.K.: Cambridge University Press, 1963), p. 186.

⁶Dorothy Sayers, *A Matter of Eternity*, ed. Rosamond Kent Sprague (Grand Rapids, Mich.: Eerdmans, 1973), p. 86.

⁷Baron Friedrich von Hügel, *Essays and Addresses on the Philosophy of Religion*, 1st series (London: J. M. Dent & Sons, 1921), pp. 216-17.

Chapter 6: Preaching

¹ *Webster's Third New International Dictionary* (Springfield, Mass.: Merriam-Webster, 1986), p. 2226.

²Søren Kierkegaard, *Attack upon Christendom, 1854-1855*, trans. Walter Lowrie (Boston: Beacon, 1944), p. 180.

³P. T. Forsyth, *The Justification of God* (London: Independent, 1917), p. 87.

Chapter 7: Prayer

¹ *The Complete Poetry and Prose of John Donne* (New York: Modern Library, 1952), p. 244.

Chapter 8: Friendship

¹Gustav Stählin, "Philos," in *Theological Dictionary of the New Testament*, ed. G. Friedrich, trans. Geoffrey W. Bromiley (Grand Rapids, Mich.: Eerdmans, 1974), 9:164.

²Søren Kierkegaard, *Søren Kierkegaard's Journals and Papers*, trans. Howard V. Hong and Edna H. Hong (Bloomington: Indiana University Press, 1970), 2:79.

³Armand M. Nicholi Jr., "The Therapist-Patient Relationship," in *The Harvard Guide to Modern Psychiatry*, ed. Armand M. Nicholi Jr. (Cambridge, Mass.: Belknap/Harvard University Press, 1978), p. 9.

⁴Ibid., p. 10.

⁵Ibid.

⁶Ibid.

⁷Ibid., p. 15.

⁸Ibid., p. 10.

⁹Jüngel, *God as the Mystery*, p. 24.

Chapter 10: Leadership

¹P. T. Forsyth, "The Ideal Ministry," *The British Congregationalist*, October 18, 1906.

²Dietrich Bonhoeffer, *Worldly Preaching*, ed. Clyde Fant (Nashville: Nelson, 1975).

³On the subject of spiritual direction I refer the reader to the works of Eugene Peterson, especially *Working the Angles: The Shape of Pastoral Integrity* (Grand Rapids, Mich.: Eerdmans, 1987).

⁴This provocative insight comes from my friend the Reverend Steven Toshio Yamaguchi.

Chapter 12: Reward

¹Leonhard Goppelt, *Theology of the New Testament*, trans. John E. Alsup (Grand Rapids, Mich.: Eerdmans, 1981), 1:122-23.